MARY 153
Mother Of the Angels

Bonnie Bee Bultman

Cover Art: Direction, Photos, and Vision Bonnie Bee Bultman.
Graphic design and layout Jacqueline Baarstad
Editor: Letter-Eye Editing Nicole Hartney
Graph Art: Heptad Repeat -Joleen Reiland-Lorenz
Graph Art: Vesica Piscis- Bonnie Bee Bultman

Permission has been given by all individuals to share their stories. To give anonymity only first
names were included in their stories.

The Gospel of Mary Magdalene by Jean-Yves Leloup published by Inner Traditions International
and Bear Company, ©2002, All Rights reserved. Reprinted with permission of publisher.

The Woman with the Alabaster Jar by Margaret Starbird published by Inner Traditions
International and

Bear Company, ©1993. All Rights reserved. Reprinted with permission of publisher.

Printed with permission of Unity, publisher of
Daily Word ®magazine.

Printed with Permission by author Margaret Starbird's use of Website Sacred Union in
Christianity and books.
Printed with permission of Scottish Rite Northern Masonic Jurisdiction

Motheroftheangels.com

TABLE OF CONTENTS

PREFACE

On July 19, 2020, I received the most beautiful gift from God: pictured proof of a rainbow lens, a portal. It wasn't until the following year that I began sharing signs of spiritual connection. Now people are sharing their signs of connection from their deceased loved ones with me. It has brought about an incredible sense of peace, love, and light.

"The eye sees only what the mind is prepared to comprehend." Henri Bergson, French Philosopher

I experienced multiple deaths of loved ones; along with listening to many people's stories about how angels have helped or even saved their lives during my life and fourteen years of forensic death investigation. My unique experiences have allowed me to focus on similarities and trends during this time, giving me a distinctive perspective at the time of someone's death. My first angel experience started with the death of my father when I was twelve years old. What happened after he died made me look closer at death, angels, and developing a strong intuition. My quest began. After a unique experience in 2007, I knew one day I would research the mysterious life of Mary Magdalene.

In 2020 COVID-19 hit, I was now a CRNA, and all elective surgeries were canceled in the United States. This gave me a once-in-a-lifetime opportunity to start writing about these experiences. My path was guided by a heavenly sign of sacred geometry, the doorway of life, and the lens of the vesica piscis—a rainbow portal connection between heaven and earth. Using my faith as the reflective lens to see the world. Guidance led me from darkness to the light when discovering the meaning of this beautiful rainbow eye, and its significance to Mary Magdalene. Her title is known as Mary H Magdalhnh, which equals 153.

My hope is that once you read *Mary 153, Mother of the Angels*, your eyes and mind will see and comprehend what your eyes may have once missed.

FORWARD

The power of prayer has forever changed my life. `In December of 2018, my decision to spend time with God each day guided me through an extraordinary journey. Prayer is an enormously powerful thing! We need the power of prayer for understanding, spiritual growth, and unity with God. This journey, for me, has twists and turns while unfolding a beautiful love story!

My life has been a journey of discovering how God works through others to communicate with us. I believe through the power of prayer, you too will have a fantastic adventure by putting prayer into practice and watching the blessings unfold in your life.

I want to give a special thank you to the following people: My mom, Marie Bultman, and my dad, Paul Bultman, for helping create the foundation of who I am today. My husband, Troy, our son, Paul, my siblings, nieces, nephews, and friends for their support during this adventure called life. Thank you to all my friends and people who were willing to share their individual experiences with me for use in *Mary 153, Mother of the Angels.*

My mom's most remarkable gifts taught me the power of prayer, the value of working hard, and having human compassion for those suffering. She was the strongest lady I have ever known, and I am immensely proud to be her daughter. She had little, and sacrificed her needs to provide for her family of seven children. The weeks that surrounded my mother's death brought about a powerful awareness of spiritual life beyond our earthly plane.

Mystifying experiences followed, which led to my desire to comprehend the mysterious life of Jesus's first apostle, Saint Mary Magdalene. Mary's life story is contentious, as are the conversations included in the Gospel of Mary with Jesus. The words are sophisticated and deeply symbolic; the importance is only understandable when applying it to your own life experiences. In 2017, long overdue, Pope Francis announced Mary Magdalene as "The Apostle to the Apostles." It is from her testimony that Christianity began.

My father, Paul, was charismatic, had great sense of humor, and his gentle nature drew people to him. He was undoubtedly the best man I have ever known, and I am blessed to know many incredibly good men. He amazed me with the things he knew about God. My dad's guidance was simple: God can hear our prayers anywhere; being in service of helping others and living our lives being a good person every day, not just on Sunday. Following these practices will lead to heaven after we die.

Life experiences after my father's death have given me powerful evidence to guide me to see how we are all connected to the energy of God and his angels. Knowledge of this helps us live the best life given the crosses we shall bear as we live our lives here on earth; or at times what may appear to be hell. My parents' deaths, along with fourteen years of forensic death investigation, provided me with a unique experience that allowed me to focus on similarities, and trends that gave me a distinctive perspective.

My personal experiences began with the death of my father when I was twelve years old. What happened after he died made me look closer at death and angels. I started to see trends in deaths, my father-in-law's death in 2003, my mother's in 2007, and my mothers-in-law's in 2016. While working in the ICU as an RN, I also saw similarities in near-death experiences or code blue events. The signs and circumstances that occurred at and around the time of death revealed a more prominent and powerful energy source as God's angels arrived to escort the patient's inner 'soul angel' across the barrier between this world and God's realm of heaven. If you have ever witnessed death, you may have felt different sensations, vibrations, or even chills before or at the time of death. Those sensations are typical when an angel is near.

My life experiences guided me to understand the power of our inner intuition. This guidance may at times come from the many angels God sends to protect and guide us. I call all of them our Guardian Angels.

I grew up with prayer in our home. I know the power of prayer through the hundreds of answered prayers I have received over my lifetime. Recently,

God made it unquestionable he was aware of what was going on in my life. At the time, I was not sure what it meant or what I would do with it. It was an incredible sign that God truly knows everything. The inner feeling became loud and prominent; without any doubt, I was to share my journey to guide others toward their abilities, which is how this book began.

I asked all my friends and family to pray for me in a broad and unspecific way, praying for the truth. In writing this book, I realized this prayer correlated to something God and the angels wanted to do. Long ago, people with foresight hid their messages to preserve history, and some items remain hidden.

Having a child has helped me realize that God loves us unconditionally; I love my son and try to stay connected to him. When I learned this, the relationship between God and humankind became more understandable. Often we do not see or have the life experiences to comprehend, but we do receive if we ask. I began to realize as a parent that the teenage years are God's way of helping us through the transition; of letting our children go to be independent and have free will. It is the same free will God has given to each of us. We can acknowledge to our children that although I love you enough to let you go, I pray that you will always love me and stay connected. God gave us the same options for independence. It makes me wonder if God is hurting because so many people have wandered away or blamed God for the evil people do in this world.

I hope this perspective may offer hope and that sharing my experiences brings an understanding that God's angels are near and ready to help answer your prayers. We are on this earth with a distinctive journey that will lead us to get to know God. Every person's journey will be different. Your story will be as unique to you as mine is to me. When I die, I will get to know all the details to fill in the missing pieces of all the things I didn't fully understand from the mystery of life. Was I close on my theories, or did I totally miss the boat?

From an early age, I never cared for the portrayal of God as something to fear or someone to instill guilt in me if I didn't follow what I viewed were countless artificial rules. I knew one day I would find something that matched more of what I was looking for and believed to be accurate based on my own experiences. I would find a place where all the people seeking

Jesus's teachings would be considered equal. A place to feel welcomed to learn about the God that is loving and kind to all his children. It would be a place of comfort, healing, safety, peace, and joy A place to discover the true love God has for all of us.

In 2007, I told my mother before she died that I hoped to one day find the teachings containing information about how we truly live our lives anchored in faith, hope, and love.

Many years ago, I became more interested in my relationship with God, which led me to try a new church. I loved the mission statement "Empowered by God to reach others for Christ." It was a game-changer for my marriage and my relationship with God. I began to see how valuable Bible teachings are in order for us to understand true-life messages. Now the messages are pouring in, and the windows and the doors have opened. As one door closes, another door opens. A door you can open too! I have learned to pray specifically and focus on what I want in life. I pray this book is a game-changer for you.

"For everyone who asks, receives; and the one who seeks, finds, and to everyone who knocks, the door will be opened." Luke 11:10

God has chosen you! What are the unique gifts given to you by God? Will you be the next physicist to solve one of the world's mysteries? A scientist to improve the quality of the food we eat? An author writing about the ingredients in food not to consume, or how to treat colony collapse disorder of honeybees? Cure more cancers? Stop osteoarthritis, chronic inflammation, or find more treatments for chronic pain? Someone to change the legal system's ability to safeguard predators who hide behind non-disclosures? Could you be the archaeologist to unearth missing pages of a full copy of The Gospel of Mary?

"So have no fear of them; for nothing is covered up that will not be uncovered, and nothing secret that will not become known." Matthew 10:26

CHAPTER 1

How God Woke Me Up!

In December, 2018, my family was in town, so we set out on an adventure to the Mall of America. It's not a place I routinely go to, but we had a fun day planned. In one of the stores, I found a selection of unique gifts amongst the clothing. I ran across several little daily calendar books and decided to buy a few as Christmas gifts for my sisters. I also found a similar book, but at the end of each story, it contained a Bible verse. I knew it would be good for me to give God some time each day for the prayers he has answered for me over the years. Although I have always been a spiritual person, I did not consider myself overly religious when it came to church or Bible teachings.

My oldest sister was on my mind when I purchased these books. She had recently had a CT scan showing an abnormal mass growing underneath her sternum. The tumor in her chest was most likely benign, but it also could be an aggressive form of cancer. The surgery required the ribs and sternum to be cut apart just like they do for an open-heart operation. She was going to have to be off work for an extended amount of time while she recovered.

My nephew was hosting Christmas for our family that year, and he had been gathering up donations from the extended family to give to a local charity. My gifts and ideas often come to me through my dreams. I had an idea from a dream the night before Christmas Eve and told my nephew we should surprise his mom, my sister, in the morning and make her the special recipient of our family's cash donations. We sent the message about the decision to help her out, so she did not have to worry about paying her bills while she was not working over the next three months. The financial peace, along with the prayer book, was the best Christmas present ever. Before her surgery, multiple people said prayers on her behalf. The prayers were quickly answered as the tumor was safely removed. It was not cancerous.

In the March of 2019, I was astonished on two consecutive days by two consecutive messages I read in the two little books I purchased four months earlier. They mysteriously detailed precisely what was occurring in my life. How ironic that after the first day, the next book, gave an even more detailed writing of what was currently going on in my life. It followed with God's advice. Be still. Lay down your sword, trust in His plan, and allow him to do the fighting. "The Lord will fight for you while you keep silent." Exodus 14:14

I was in complete shock! The irony of buying this book several months ago; the type of book I would have never purchased before. Then the successive messages revealing exactly what was going on in my life was incredibly strange and mysterious all at the same time. I had no idea why, other than it was a way of God letting me know that he knew what was going on in my life. The coincidence of the timing is what I found the most incredible. It comes down to looking at the circumstances of why and when it occurred. Everyone has bad days and can relate to messages. This was a blessing. What might be a dreadful day in life is a good day for the soul.

Fast forward to September 5, 2019, the message was about asking God to uncover hidden expectations in my heart as well as discovering the source of these messages. I prayed to set myself free from any expectations that were not really from him.

I did not want anything to come from a negative source of energy. I prayed and prayed to have something revealed to me. Three days later, on the morning of Sunday, September 8, 2019, I texted my sister telling her I was struggling with the message I had read three days prior. It was after I sent her the text that my husband and I watched a new online series called *Divine Direction*.

I knew right away that God was working through the pastor to answer the question in my prayers. What do I need to do to start? If you want answers;

fast and pray. With the help of Amanda Rose's *Eat Like a Bear,* I was doing intermittent fasting. (Go Bears!)

When you live by faith, you don't ignore the facts. Why is this happening? What are the facts? The moment you decide to fight a problem or stand up for the truth and attempt something honorable, brace for opposition. The pastor spoke about the moment you stand up for truth, you will be falsely accused, and someone will oppose you. The moment you stand up for the truth, this is going to happen to you! One of the signs that tells us when something is the right thing to do is that someone will criticize you. How many people will turn against you when you are doing what God has called for you to do? Holy shit, finally someone who understands!

The pastor continued telling a story about author John Grisham, who started writing one page a day, and after a year, he had a novel. Grisham, a former lawyer, no longer practices law but is a best-selling author.

"God's grace is all you need. God's power is made perfect in weakness, so I delight in my weaknesses because when I am weak, then I am strong." 2 Corinthians 12:9-10

I have been told most of my life to write a book about my time working as a forensic death investigator and my perspective on death. I always thought it would be a good murder mystery thriller, but the message was very emotional for me. Tears ran down my cheeks and I knew it was the answer to the question I was praying for, but not the one I thought I would receive that day. Writing has always been my greatest weakness. The thought of writing a book scared me. Few things scare me, but writing a book is no easy task! I know happiness will be on the other side of my fear. I have always worked extremely hard to achieve my goals once I can see the vision. "My grace is sufficient for you, for my power is made perfect in weakness." 2 Corinthians 12:9-10

On this same day, September 8, 2019, I was stunned as my sister responded to my text with a copy from the Daily Word. It was called Guidance – I wait peacefully for guidance. *Each time I ask for guidance, I place my trust in the Spirit. By consciously taking this step, I open my mind and heart to receive. I clear away concerns clouding my receptivity and shift my focus toward divine love and light. I ignore discouraging words from others because I have gone directly to the source of wisdom. As I wait, I do not fall asleep by restricting the way which guidance comes. It reaches me in many ways, perhaps through something I hear, see, read, or feel deep within. I maintain a faithful watch, for I know answers are available, and my way will be made clear. I already feel lighter—the first blessing of more to come. I give thanks in advance as I wait peacefully.*

It was astonishing; the message my sister sent me was dated with the same date! Was this serendipity or synchronicity? Some people say there are no coincidences however I had never had this many things being presented so blatantly to me before.

According to the Divine Direction message referenced Acts 1:8: You will receive power "when the Holy Spirit has come upon you, you will tell people about me, everywhere—In Jerusalem, throughout Judea, in Samaria, and to the ends of the Earth." To whom much is given, much is required!" (Eagle Brook Church)

Two days later was the icing on the cake for me. Throughout my entire life, my prayers, vision, and knowledge have become solidified at night. My dreams have awakened me between 3:17 a.m. to 5:00 a.m. for a long time now to the point, I finally kept a notebook by the bed to record everything that happened.

On September 10, 2019, a note on Dreams from Daily Word was again sent to me by my sister. It read, *"My dreams came true as I put them into action." It was not enough for me simply to hope a dream will come true—I must take action! The place to begin is always with God. I turn to my spiritual source in prayer. In silence, I give my desires to God and listen with an open heart and mind to the inspiration that comes to me. I remember that God's guidance comes in all forms and often from unexpected places. These signs and wonders might confuse me, but I trust I am on my perfect path. I follow my guidance as I move in the direction of my dreams. Joel 2:28 "Then it will come about at a later time that I will pour out my Spirit on every person. Your sons and your daughters will prophesy. Your older people will dream dreams, and your young people will see visions."*

The messages poured in, but it was unbelievable to comprehend how this many things could all be lining up simultaneously. I would never deny

4

the power; I kept notes of everything happening while continuing to pray that the source of this was genuinely coming from God. On September 15, 2019, my husband and I attended a church service. The Divine Direction series contained Proverbs 3:5-6 "Trust in the Lord with all your heart; do not depend on your understanding. Seek his will in all you do, and he will show you which path to take." After the service, I told my husband I wanted to have prayers said for God is the source of the messages. I went to speak to the pastor. I showed him the original pages from the books, the dates in March and now September. He asked if someone had sent that to me. I said no, not all three, it was from two books I bought back in December 2018. I asked him if he could pray for the source being truly from God and that I would know the truth and he would continue to guide me to understand why I was receiving them. He said the church had a prayer group, and he would add my request to the group. I thanked him and left.

I began to pray for a more specific direction; more information began to come my way. I started to journal a more detailed timeline of occurrences, documenting every amazing sign in my life. I had long put off many of my unique experiences and memories that are stored in my limbic system. The limbic system is a set of structures in the brain that controls emotions and stores memories. It contains regions that detect fear, controls the body's functions, and perceives sensory information. It is here in the brain that connection can be made between smells, memories, and feelings. For example, the scent of cinnamon is a fond memory as it reminds me of my mom's homemade apple pie at Christmas time. The limbic system can also store bad memories as well. Sometimes stored memories can have a way of creeping out of us, and unconsciously, we may not even understand why we are getting so upset. A simple little trigger may unlock or bring you back to those memories of anger, fear, or other negative sensations.

Luckily, there are now new therapies to deal with and resolve the trapped memories. One therapy is called Eye Movement Desensitization and Reprocessing (EMDR). EMDR is a technique where the trauma is recalled by doing side-to-side eye movement or hand tapping. The rapid rhythmic eye movements dampen the power of the emotionally charged memories of these past traumatic events and eventually minimizes the physiological response on the body if triggered. It is lovely to have tools to help people who have post-traumatic stress disorder (PTSD), and it also has good results for those who suffer from anxiety. I saw this therapy work for someone who had had PTSD. I decided to try this tool, and it ended up being another big piece to saving my marriage. I had no fuse left for specific behaviors that would open the flood gates of twenty-plus years of irritation resulting in a lot of anger. I am incredibly grateful that this tool was available to prevent the past from affecting me now because today is all we have. Every day is a gift; that is why it is called the present. I know God answers in his own time, not the earthly time we are used to, so now I live in the present and wait for his guidance as this story unfolds.

CHAPTER 2

God Has a Funny Sense of Humor

God has a sense of humor. Because the thought of me writing a book is extremely funny! I am terrible at spelling and my grammar is bad. My senior year of high school was a blessing on how to become more successful in the future. After reading my paper my English teacher, Joan, asked me how I made it to my senior year of high school not knowing how to use punctuation? I shrugged my shoulders and smiled at her because I knew I never understood English, but somehow I passed, and here I am, ta-dah! I told myself I am NEVER going to need this skill in my future! Oh, how wrong I was. I laugh now as I write this. I now know that Joan stopping me that day was an early blessing for my future. She said as you navigate college, you will need to go to the tutoring office because you have a learning disability. You do not put your words down on paper correctly. She advised me to have my documents reviewed by a tutor before turning them in. Her advice and blessing were right on the mark. I made it through college following Joan's direction. I was ecstatic to have received a B in my first college English class. WOW!

I also received some advice from a high school counselor, discouraging me from taking anything complex or challenging in college. That advice to me was total bullshit! Schools did not realize there are many different learning styles, and you only need to figure out your personal learning style to become successful. It took me a little while to learn my learning style, but I did it! Perseverance is the key to accomplishing any goal and dream. Can you imagine letting that negative counselor influence me versus the positive teacher who told me how to be successful? My life could have been vastly different. In my first job following college, I was a forensic death investigator for the Hennepin County Medical Examiner's Office, which included the city of Minneapolis, MN. For every death I had to write their story. Are you kidding me now! I was not supposed to need to know how to write. Oh, thank God for spell-check!

I had a great female colleague who was a friend and a personal cheerleader. Linda started teaching me simple English and grammatical differences to help me become a better writer. Over the years, we have had many good laughs over my errors. When I was writing a patient's past medical history, she had labile diabetes. At the end of my report, I would always hit the spell-check. My labile diabetes (meaning brittle and elevated blood sugars) was now labial (lips) diabetes. All the investigators, managers, and physicians gathered in a large conference room for a case review in the morning. We all read the cases and went over what was still needed to close the case. Dr. Peterson, the Chief Medical Examiner at the time, read my report and said, "Oh, Sweetlips." Everyone roared, including me! I chose to laugh at my weakness. Knowing this was one of my weaknesses, I have worked most of my adult life to become a better writer. Although I had many people telling me to write a book about my experiences, I never believed I could.

My husband, Troy, is very well read. Not to mention extremely good-looking, tall, dark, and handsome. He has never put me down for my weakness and has always helped me on projects. Both of us have a good sense of humor. I grew up in Fargo, North Dakota. The film *Fargo* really brought out how we speak to the world! "You betcha!" is probably known worldwide from *Fargo*. My husband was interviewing with his chief for a promotion. One of his questions was, do you speak any foreign languages? He replied, "Yes, Fargoanese!" The chief looked at him with a puzzled look. He answered my wife is from Fargo, they speak a different language, and I can communicate with them. They laughed as the chief took a couple of notes and moved on.

When I overcame my weaknesses, it no longer held me back from doing more challenging things. It allowed me to have more confidence and achieve goals. Long ago, it became apparent to me that people who try to put someone down or focus on other people's faults are simply insecure. This negative focus can be tough to break. I try to stay positive while not letting it affect my ability to shine.

The second book of Corinthians 12:9 describes our ability to trust God and have confidence in his timing, tying it to our willingness to set aside our skills, abilities, and ingenuity. We trade our weakness for his strength. Paul boasted of his weakness because it brought God into his life with incredible power. Paul became an empty vessel, and Christ lived through him, accomplishing amazing things. This great privilege is open to all of us. Only when we empty ourselves of our ego can we be filled with something better. When we are weak, then we can become strong. Sometimes we pray for strength when God wants us to remain in our weakness, dependent upon him. These weaknesses are perfecting us so that Christ's divine power can be revealed through the window of our human weakness.

It is in these times when our beautiful lives break, and we put them back together that we finally see the true light of God through these cracks! This happened to the entire world in 2020! Our beautiful lives broke apart so we could once again see God.

CHAPTER 3

My First Angel Experience

I had grown up a Daddy's Girl. I was the grand finale, the seventh child born in the seventh month of the year. My mom, who wanted her kitchen redone, said when she thought she might be pregnant again at the age of forty-one, "this better be a tumor!" I told her she just saved the best for last! My dad was forty-eight at the time. He said I would be a girl, and we would name her Bonnie Bee after the honeybee. My dad knew things about the future, like the fact I would have a lot of brown hair and brown eyes. Everyone disagreed as all my siblings were bald at birth, but my dad was right! I came out with brown eyes and thick locks of golden-brown hair. My unique middle name makes me proud as it was something special my dad intended just for me.

Ironically, the honeybee is a symbol of good luck, wealth, and prosperity. It is the world's most important pollinator of food crops. Einstein predicted that when bees disappeared off the earth, man would only have four years to live. Colony collapse disorder (CCD) is a mysterious disease sweeping through US and European honeybee hives. CCD is a phenomenon that occurs when many of the worker bees in the colony disappear, leaving the queen and a few nurse bees to care for the remaining immature bees. CCD has been occurring since 2006. The disorder affects the adult bees' ability to navigate. They leave the hive to find pollen and never return. Some causes of CCD are in-hive insects, mite control, and exposure to pesticides applied to crops. Globally more honeybees exist than other types of bee pollinating insects. Approximately a third of the food we eat each day relies on pollination from bees. Birds, bats, and insects also pollinate, but not to the same extent. I read an interesting article once that said honeybees can remember faces. A honeybee's brain has a million neurons, compared with eighty-six billion in a human brain. Bees are fond of humans that take loving care of them. With the ability to recognize their caretaker's face, they build trust with humans. This good memory serves them well to remember where they can find pollen and nectar. BEE KIND!

Dad

My dad had an entrepreneurial spirit and owned his own real estate business. He did both residential and rural real estate. His office was attached to the front of our home, allowing him to work from home and for me to see him every day. I was fortunate to have lived in the same house my entire childhood. As an infant, I was baptized in the living room of our home. Our home had beautiful dark woodwork, wooden French doors, four beautiful wooden windows framing the living room's front wall. His office had a similar mirrored set of windows out the front of the house. Dad's office was one of my favorite places; it was bright, painted yellow, and received the east and the southern sunshine. It was a cozy place to be with my dad.

I often accompanied my dad on his travels to see farmland he had listed for sale or go out to one of our two farms. It was back before seatbelts were required and I would sit next to him in the front bench seat, and he would let me steer the car down the highway. Once we got out near our farmland, he would let me get out and run alongside the car just to see how fast I could go. We didn't have a lot of money, but we did have a lot of high-quality memories. Being outside is where we loved to be together. We spent a lot of time at our farms doing a family garden. It is funny, I still remember picking rocks from the farmed fields, however, our primary home was in the city.

The Storm

One of my fondest memories of my dad was during a storm. My dad and I would go to the door to listen and watch them. Still to this to this day I enjoy the memories of watching a good storm roll through. I knew my dad found peace in storms. I have always loved the water; it is so majestic, hearing rain or crashing waves against the shore. It was not until I started my journey in December 2018 that I began reading scripture and finally knew why.

"The voice of the LORD is over the waters; the God of glory thunders, the Lord is upon many waters." Psalm 29:3

Now I wish I could only ask him what he was thinking of during those times when we watched the storms together.

Kind, Strong, Intelligent, and Humorous

Growing up, I was surrounded by kind, strong, intelligent, and humorous men, resulting in me being the same kind of woman. I was never afraid of a man's world. At an early age, I learned adult humor. Having humor in your life is especially important. My dad and I loved to laugh! He had countless one-liners and a plethora of funny jokes. When I didn't have school the next day, I would watch late-night television with my dad. *The Tonight Show* starring Johnny Carson, or *The Benny Hill Show*, were a couple of our favorites. Being around my dad and this type of humor gave me a better understanding of a man's dialogue, which helped me be successful in some of my careers where predominately men worked.

My mom was a nurse who worked the three to eleven shift. I didn't see her much, so my dad let me play tricks on her when it was not a school night. I would hide in the back seat of the car in my effort to scare her once she got in as I jumped up. It was hard not being able to see her very much. I remember crawling into my mom's bed in the morning for a few minutes just to see her before I was off to school. Saturdays mom and I would bake. I usually spilled something on my shirt while baking, no matter how hard I tried. I still do that sometimes now, bringing back those fond memories.

Sunday mornings, we would all go to church. My mom had never driven, so my dad would drop the whole family off at church. I asked my dad why he didn't go to church with the rest of us. He said because he believed that we needed to be good people every day of our lives. He didn't like that some people in church would sit in the front row, but they were not such good people once they left church. It was not until much later in my life that I learned the Catholic Church wouldn't marry my parents in front of the altar. After dropping his family off, my dad used to attend a different church by himself. My dad was the most beautiful person I have ever known in my life. It breaks my heart to think of the time we did not spend together as a family because he was not welcome by the church we attended. It was the ultimate oxymoron. God loves everyone equally, but here we have specific rules that apply.

Colorado

It was the fall of 1981. I remember my dad taking a trip out to Colorado with his sister. It seemed odd that no one else from our family went along even though it was a place he had always wanted to visit. Dad drove a prominent golden-colored Chrysler New Yorker. I remember how sad I was that he was leaving on this trip because I had spent every day of my life with my dad in some fashion to this point. I stood in the street watching as he drove down the road taking the first turn to the right until his car went out of sight. It was the last memory of my dad as a healthy person. When my dad returned from his trip to Colorado, he was extremely sick. He told us how he was traveling over a large bridge when he suddenly couldn't breathe. He went to see a new doctor as his primary doctor was out of town. The doctor took a chest x-ray and scheduled him for a lung biopsy. I was alone with him in the living room when he started to have trouble breathing. He was coughing and couldn't catch his breath. I asked if he wanted me to get mom. He shook his head no. He continued to cough and gasp for air. I could see the change of color to his skin and yelled, "MOMMMMM!" She quickly came into the living room, and I ran outside. Thank goodness my friend was walking by at the time. I was in tears as I didn't know if my dad would be alive or dead when I went back inside.

When I returned, he looked much better; blue was not a good color on him. I sat down next to him on the couch; I was only twelve years old at the time. I remember asking him if he was afraid to die. He said time is much different in heaven than it is here on earth. He assured me that it would not be that long until the day we would all be together in heaven.

I now research what he shared with me at the age of twelve. Many years later, I found the biblical reference. "Beloved, do not forget this one thing, that with the Lord one day is like a thousand years, and a thousand years are like one day" 2 Peter 3:8. Doctors and Lawyers must have similar calendars to God.

Mental toughness

Coincidentally my dad also knew that he would not live to see 1982. He was diagnosed with non-small cell carcinoma of the lung, which had metastasized to his bone. One day he was standing in the kitchen, and sneezed, breaking his hip. He then spent many days in the hospital. I was in seventh grade middle school at the time and my father was the only driver between my parents, so I would walk the distance to school when he was sick. No, it was not uphill both ways! After school, I played basketball. I was on the undefeated seventh-grade girls basketball team. After my games and practices, I walked miles to the hospital to see my dad each night. It was a bittersweet situation. I loved basketball, but my parents could never attend a single game. Winter had begun, and it was the first time I realized just how strong my mind was. I had been up at the hospital with my dad and two older sisters. My sisters asked me to step outside the room while they helped my dad with his care. I didn't see why I had to leave the room, so I asked for my winter jacket. After asking for it three times, my sister wouldn't give it to me. I chose to leave walking miles home in my jeans and a short-sleeved shirt. I kept telling myself the whole way home, "you're not cold, you're not cold!" I really wouldn't recommend this to anyone as Fargo winters are frigid and windy! It was the first time I pushed my mind on mental toughness and I learned that positive self-talk is a valuable tool to use to accomplish goals.

Eventually, we brought my dad home to let him die in the comfort of his own home. We set up a hospice bed where our sofa and end table usually sat. My dad asked if he could have the Anointing of the Sick as he knew his death was imminent. My oldest sister called the Catholic Church to perform the sacrament before my dad died. The Father initially said they couldn't do it because he was not an official member. I remember my sister, Helen, replying, "Father, I have a question for you. The church teaches us how God is loving and forgiving. Who are you to deny a man who has been nothing but a good man his entire life?" The Father said he would call back. Once he returned the call, he told us he had found a loophole! He came to perform the Anointing of the Sick on my dad, just as he requested.

I recall sitting with my dad while my family had dinner, holding his cold hand. I hated that feeling, so I tried to warm him up. Later that evening, the family gathered around him, offering love and comfort. My mom's sister was a nun, and she led a prayer of the rosary. My rosary was wrapped in my dad's hand. I was sitting in the chair where my dad would usually sit to watch television. My sister's cat, who would typically be hiding, was sitting at the top of my chair. Kitty meowed three times at the time of my dad's death, and my dad had a tear that rolled down his cheek as his inner soul angel left us. He died in the first hour of Thursday, December 31, 1981. Less than twenty-four hours away from 1982. Again, as he predicted, he did not live to see the year 1982.

Everyone was able to be there except one of my brothers. My brother, Gary, shared how he woke up to a very odd feeling and sensation. He got up from his bed to shake off the feeling, but as he returned to his bed, he saw an image of my dad in his window smiling at him. He said a calming feeling came over him as the image gradually became increasingly distant until the image was miles away, then eventually disappeared.

My nephew Mike was only five years old and was very sick the night of my dad's death. In the morning when my sister told her son that his grandpa had died last night. Mike replied grandpa was just here standing in the doorway. As an adult, Mike still can recall vividly the image of him standing in the doorway. My dad traveled to see his son and grandson before his inner soul angel left this earthly plane.

When I woke up, I came down into our living room in the morning. I stood in front of our beautifully decorated Christmas tree, feeling numb as I remember thinking I could not ever imagine living five years without my dad. My most profound regret was never saying to my dad how much I loved him. The love language in our home was an act of service. We showed you how much we loved you by doing nice things, but we never verbalized it. It is slightly better today with my siblings. We said I love you once and I'll let you know if anything changes!

The funeral was on Saturday, January 2. Our family events usually involve some major weather events, and on this day, there was a big snowstorm.

My First Angel

Sunday, January 3, 1982, just three days after my dad's death, I became ill. Our sofa was now back in its usual spot against the south wall in the living room. Drifting in and out of sleep, I remember lying there alone and needing help. No one was there to help me because they had all gone to church. I remember saying if my dad had not died, he would have been there to help me as he never went to their church.

The next thing I remember was the most vivid dream that I can still see today. A giant golden shining circular sphere of light came down through the windows of my dad's front office and the living room windows of our house. It went from the ceiling to the floor. I have no other memories after it entered the room.

I know I was ill for a while and did not return to school after winter break because of the illness. When I did go back to school, it sucked! No one would talk to me. I'm sure people didn't know what to say to me. My home economics teacher was the only person I recall giving me sympathy at school. Maybe others did, too, but I don't remember because I was in a fog. I lost all my close friendships within a year; only one or two remained. I have very few memories of this time in my life other than crying myself to sleep every night due to the tremendous pain in my heart. At night I would pray. I knew I could never kill myself, so I simply prayed that the world would end. I prayed this every night for a long time. Thank God for some unanswered prayers!

The fog remained for about a year and a half. I was in ninth grade and walking home from school when suddenly my ears popped. It was excruciating but quickly went away. I immediately knew that the sphere or bubble had burst! I remember the exact location when they popped, and my memory came back with considerable detail. This was an angel or some form of protective mechanism. I have vivid memories from when I was a young child sitting on my potty chair in the bathroom, but few memories for the year and a half following my dad's death. I believe this golden sphere carried me through this horrific time in my life. Looking back, this time resonates with a poem.

"FOOTPRINTS IN THE SAND" One night, a man had a dream. He dreamed he was walking along the beach with the LORD. Across the sky flashed scenes from his life. For each scene, he noticed two sets of footprints in the sand: one belonging to him and the other to the LORD. When the last scene of his life flashed before him, he looked back at the footprints in the sand. He noticed that many times along the path of his life, there was only one set of footprints. He also noticed that it happened at the lowest and saddest times in his life. This really bothered him, and he questioned the LORD about it. "LORD, you said that once I decided to follow you, you'd walk with me all the way. But I have noticed that during the most troublesome times in my life, there is only one set of footprints. I don't understand why when I needed you most, you would leave me." The LORD replied, "My precious, precious child, I love you, and I would never leave you. During your times of trial and suffering, when you see only one set of footprints, it was then that I carried you."

It was after this my love of angels grew, and I knew they were always around me.

The Music Box

On the third anniversary following my dad's death, my brother, John, and I were watching TV in the living room. I was lying on the floor when our music box spontaneously began to play. The music box with two beautiful Christmas doves on it didn't play for long, but after it stopped, I looked at my brother and we both smiled. We knew it was our dad! The music box sat on an end table next to the sofa in the same corner our dad had died. The clock above the chair where my brother was sitting displayed the same time our dad had died three years prior.

This experience started my quest to learn more about the spiritual world and what happens when we die. Interestingly, we both knew immediately that this was a sign from our dad. Before my dad died, I often knew when my dad was coming home by an internal feeling and a particular smell that made me aware of him. This is because I was so connected to his inner soul angel's vibrational energy. I had the exact experience after he died, and I knew instantly it was him. If you talk to someone who has lost a loved one and they see a particular sign that may trigger them to know precisely who it is from, this comes from their subconscious brain remembering that person's vibrational energy. Try it for yourself. Certain things such as cardinals, eagles, feathers, and pennies from heaven will often remind people of a loved one. Ask them who it is from, and they will know precisely because they will subconsciously feel that spirit's vibrational energy guiding these animals to get their attention.

Everything in the universe is made up of energy and matter, which vibrates at different frequencies. Energetic vibrations can even attract similar vibrations. All vibrations operate at high and low frequencies. Humans can sense mechanical oscillations ranging in frequency from below 1 hertz (Hz) to 100 hertz. Here on earth, we are in lower frequencies. For example, our brain waves function between .5 to 42 Hz. We are exposed to higher frequencies, leading to general annoyance and discomfort. The heavenly plane operates at a higher frequency. Angels can emanate vibrations to help you. Have you ever had a sudden, powerful, yet uncomfortable feeling? It may be your guardian angel's way of having you pay attention to something. They are getting remarkably close to your inner circle of energy. Depending on how close they are to you, it may vary in the degree or the level of discomfort. Many call this your intuition. Your angels are always around you, guiding you and trying to keep you safe. You may always call on your angels for protection. I am blessed to have many angels in my life.

Most owners of animals acknowledge that their animal will sense the vibrational energy long before people do. Animals may look over your shoulder into the next room. Animals can hear sounds as high as 47,000 to 65,000 Hz. Stop and try to notice if you feel any sensations. It may come as a chill or a generalized uncomfortableness or even at times an irritating feeling. Over time, by paying closer attention to these vibrations, you will be more aware of when your guardian angels are near or trying to send you a message.

A lady once indicated that her dog charged into her breast with such force and wouldn't leave her alone. She noted an ache and felt a lump in her breast. Seeking medical treatment, she had the lump removed and was diagnosed with breast cancer. Animals can help as they can hear and respond to the higher heavenly frequencies.

Some people may say that domestic and wild animals have a sixth sense as they can hear and feel the vibrations long before humans can. Once we realize that animals can be directed by an angel's vibrational frequency, the guidance will become clearer for us to pay attention to.

One of the most amazing animal stories on this topic was on December 26, 2004. A 9.1 magnitude earthquake triggered a deadly tsunami in the Indian Ocean hitting the popular tourist areas of Sri Lanka and Thailand. Reports indicate that elephants screamed and ran for higher ground, and flamingos abandoned their low-lying breeding grounds before the tsunami hit. Survivors state they ran and followed the animals' paths to higher ground, saving their lives. Over 200,000 people died from the deadly tsunami, but few animals are noted to have died. On the same day, a dog owner said their dogs refused to go on their daily beach run. It ended up saving their lives. The animals were guided by the vibrational frequency of where to go. No animal fled towards the beach. If the animals could feel the vibrations from the earthquake, how does it explain that they knew which direction to go for safety? The answer is that they were guided by the angels to safety

CHAPTER 4

The Soul's Energy Contained
in the Human Body

The brain is the center hub of electrical activity. The cells in the brain, called neurons, send electrical signals to other neurons in the body. These brain waves of electrical energy are measured by frequency cycles per second or hertz and range from slow to fast. The electroencephalogram (EEG) is a printed recording of the electrical activity of the brain. The patterns are called brain waves. The brain wave is an oscillation of electrical potential contained in large sheaths of neural tissue found throughout our bodies.

There are five different brain waves measured by the electroencephalogram EEG.

1) Delta Waves is the smallest at .5 to 4 Hz. They are present when sleeping, dreaming, and in awake infant and comatose patients. Adequate levels of delta waves help the immune system's natural healing and feeling of rejuvenation after a deep sleep. Seven to nine hours of sleep is crucial for promoting human growth hormone release and muscle recovery if you are working to change your physique. Seven to nine hours of sleep further allows for four to five complete sleep cycles to occur, promoting good health. Melatonin is a hormone released from the pineal gland at night and gradually decreases with age and is also associated with antiaging. Suppose

you are having trouble getting enough sleep. In that case, one may want to look at their blue light exposure from devices as it suppresses the body's natural release of melatonin, especially before you plan to go to sleep. Some eyeglasses can help block blue light wave exposure if you spend much time on a computer or phone.

2) Theta Waves 4-8 Hz occur in a deeply relaxed state and in meditation.

3) Alpha Waves 8-12 Hz are present when we are very relaxed, or in a state of passive attention or meditation. Some research states you may increase alpha brain waves if you put your mind to it. Neurofeedback training has helped some people with generalized anxiety disorders to increase their amplitude of alpha waves, giving them an increased sense of calm and decreasing anxiety. Relaxation techniques like mindfulness and meditation increase alpha waves, helping the body feel more peaceful, less anxious and may even boost creativity levels.

4) Beta Waves 12-35 Hz are present when awake and the mind is active.

5) Gamma Waves 35-42 Hz occur when concentrating and problem-solving.

When the energy of our inner soul angel leaves the human body, the EEG will have no electroactivity, and the person will die or be declared brain dead. Modern medicine can now keep the body's functions alive for a brief period following brain death to allow for a donation of vital organs to give life to someone in need.

The brainstem is deep within the brain; it has a critical role in regulating heart rate, breathing, sleeping, and eating. All information relayed between the brain and the body must pass through the brain stem. Interestingly, the limbic system of the brain lies around the superior portion of the brainstem. The limbic system is the emotional brain and houses the structures that display elevated neural activity levels during emotional experiences. This area is the midbrain; on either side are the right and left hemispheres. At the bottom is the corpus callosum which connects both halves and delivers messages from one half of the brain to another.

THE SOUL'S ENERGY CONTAINED IN THE HUMAN BODY

The brainstem is the hub of the superhighway connection from the brain to the spinal cord and sends messages to the rest of the body including the heart. It was once believed that the creation of neurons stopped shortly after birth. Brain plasticity or neuroplasticity refers to the brain's ability to change and adapt because of experience. Neurogenesis is the creation of new neurons! What are the seven methods to boost brain plasticity?

(1) BEE open to change and education
(2) Get regular exercise
(3) BEE Creative
(4) M&Ms (Meditate & Music)
5) Eat a healthy diet
6) Get plenty of sleep
7) BEE The Light! Positive! Laughter!

These activities will get the creative energy flowing throughout your body.

The human body is full of energy; even some of the individual cells within the body contain voltage-gated channels. The plasma membrane of all the electrically excitable cells—not only neurons but also endocrine, muscles, and egg cells—includes the voltage-gated cation channels responsible for generating the action potentials. They use cellular energy (ATP) to pump the ions against their concentration gradient.

The flow of energy is also evident in the heart. The heart contains specialized cells called pacemakers which discharge electrical impulses that initiate the heartbeat. The action potential is a rapid surge of electrical activity. It fires quickly changing the voltage from the inside and outside of the cell membrane, as it continues to travel as propagating waves through the heart's walls, prompting the heart muscle to contract and produce a beat. A pumping heart sends oxygenated blood to the rest of the body's cells. Once the heart has no more signals from the brainstem, it will cease its activity, and the human body dies.

Energy from the body known as our soul, or inner soul angel leaves and is transformed into a different energy configuration. Everyone has a piece of this energy given to them by God connecting us all. The inner soul angel's energy can stay connected or give you signals through vibrational waves. The waves can come through by light or sound.

Acoustic Energy

Ultrasound waves are created by converting electrical energy into acoustic energy. Because the travel time for sound waves is incredibly fast, it allows for rapid successive waves to be sent, received, and processed fast enough to create an illusion or image in real-time. The human ear cannot hear ultrasound waves. Ultrasound is how one gets a picture of an unborn baby. Ultrasound refers to the use of sound waves from 2 to 15 MHz (megahertz = one million cycles per second.) The human ear can interpret sound waves in a range of 20 to 20,000 hertz.

Ultrasound is a tool used to see internal anatomy by people performing anesthesia to place local anesthetics blocking the body's ability to send the brain pain signals. This results in no pain for a duration of time. The ultrasound probe contains piezoelectric material housed inside the ultrasound probe; a shape change occurs and causes it to vibrate. The piezoelectric effect is the cornerstone of traditional ultrasound. An electromechanical property like quartz is a natural piezoelectric substance when an electrical current applied through the object generates vibrations resulting in pulsed sound waves. The return effect are echoes reflected on the crystal to create a change in electrical resistance and current. Every time the sound waves pass through a different medium, the beam is refracted, and some of the waves change direction as well as velocity resulting in an image or picture.

Refraction is the change in the direction of a wave caused by the difference in the wave's speed. Examples of this are sound and light waves. Diverse types of mediums include air and water. Quartz crystals or glass used in ultrasounds are also one of the materials used in a camera lens. Quartz could be the plausible reason the camera lens can pick up electrical sound waves or lines of light, capturing images of the inner soul angel's energy in pictures. Quartz crystals also maintain a precise frequency standard, which helps regulate the movement of a clock or watch, making timepieces perfectly accurate.

CHAPTER 5

Good Angels Sent by God to Help
Believers Hebrews 1:14

Angels possess intelligence from God. They are the messengers of divine messages and warn or encourage in times of danger and care for the righteous at the time of death. Angel stories are numerous throughout the world; they are written about in every religion, and their presence is felt by many.

There are ten distinct types of orders of angels. The first three or four seem to be the ones most connected to us here on earth. Depending on the source, the definition of what each angel does may vary. It will be one of those questions I get answered on the other side for clarification. Here is a generalized guideline for the different angels referenced in the world and biblical writings.

(1) **Guardian angels** are the ones we are the most familiar with and feel connected to on earth as they are here to protect and guide us. Guardian angels work as God's messengers to us. Although guardian angels are the furthest away from God, they are remarkably close to us here on earth. At various times you may be able to feel their presence around you through their vibrational frequencies. God has given us these angels to help us through our demanding lives and follow our true path until they escort us to heaven. Guardian angels work in mysterious ways and can often direct help and guidance through animals here on earth.

(2) **Archangels** are often the most recognized and mean "chief angel." Gabriel is God's primary messenger, and Archangel Michael is the Guardian and a holy fighter. Michael is often the most recognized Archangel. The Archangels help us when we need hope; they can send messages for us to others. Have you ever been praying for a specific request, and it suddenly happens? This was your angel sending your message to answer your prayers. Archangel Raphael is known to facilitate healing through superhuman physical knowledge to heal the sick.

(3) **Principalities angels**. These angels are rays of light who oversee all things. They are rays of golden sunshine that give us an instant connection to God. They guide the world and cities to look after politics (they must be swamped now or short-staffed with such a divide going on in the world.) They also help send other angels on missions to help protect humans who are in danger.

(4) **Powers** are giant angels using their electrical force to protect and heal you. They are closely related to the Holy Spirit and help us overcome temptations. The Powers are said to work through the power of love in healers, musicians, artists, scientists, and physicists.

(5) **Virtues** help to keep order in all things. They are the ones that remove the negative energies in the world and individuals that try to keep us from making the right choice. They are known as purity and considered royalty. Miracles can be associated with the angels of Virtues and can also help us recognize that God exists.

(6) **Carrions** only have one mission: to carry away dark entities when they die, so no dark entities exist on the earth after they have died.

(7) **Dominions** are heavenly governors, trying to find the balance between matter, spirit, good and evil.

(8) **Cherubim** radiate with the light of the knowledge of God. Their name, "cherubim" means "great understanding" or "effusion of wisdom" in Hebrew because it is thought the cherubim wisdom is sent down infusing the

knowledge from God. Harmony is the state where God's work and plan follows the correct course.

(9) **Seraphim** are aflame with love. They are the closest angels to God. In Hebrew, Seraphim means "flaming."

(10) **Thrones** are angel keepers of celestial records and hold the knowledge of God. They are responsible for sticking to the Divine Will, known as God's plan.

CHAPTER 6

The Messenger of the Mysteries of God

Gabriel means "God is my strength." Gabriel the Archangel is the messenger of the mysteries of God, especially the incarnation of God and all other mysteries related to it. God sent the angel Gabriel to Mary with the message she would have a son, whom she was to name Jesus. However, Joseph was informed about Jesus in a dream. The world holds many mysteries, while some mysteries now have scientific knowledge that explains how they work. The following are a few mysteries I believe are relevant to the abilities of angels here on earth.

Rainbows are a magnificent gift from God. There are seven colors to the rainbow, and the colors always appear in the same order in a spectrum of red, orange, yellow, green, blue, indigo, and violet. An easy reference to remember the order is ROY G BIV. In ancient Greece, rainbows were believed to be the paths or portals made for the messengers of the gods as they traveled between heaven and earth. Buddhists believe at the time of death the body transcends to a form known as the rainbow body or body of light; a sign of ascension towards God or the bridge connecting the two planes through the seven colors. Scientifically we know rainbows form as sunlight shines on droplets of moisture in the earth's atmosphere. The droplets act like prisms, refracting or separating light into colors and sending them off in a range of angles between 40 and 42 degrees from the opposite direction to the sun. This explanation was discovered by physicist Isaac Newton. My theory is both are correct, as spiritual energy may contain moisture, resulting in spheres or orbs with a rainbow edge, capturing the energies of light in photos. Several people including myself, have now captured the rainbow portals when sensing a spiritual connection to a loved one's spirit that has traveled to heaven. There are incredible photos of proof captured all over the world.

The other interesting fact is your brain interprets the various energies of visible light as assorted colors. These range from red having the lowest energy (but the longest wavelength), to violet which has the highest energy (but the shortest wavelength) because light, is a wave.

The happiest color is yellow. It is linked to the psychological powers of sunlight to lift our mood, improve our outlook on life, and be life's energy source here on earth. These positive effects stimulate the nervous system. The other reason yellow has mood-lifting effects is the ability of yellow to stand out from assorted colors on the spectrum. Yellow's ability to stand out helps to associate yellow with positive memories.

Spooky Action at a Distance

Quantum entanglement, or what Albert Einstein referred to as "spooky action at a distance," is a phenomenon by which one particle can effectively *know* something about another particle instantaneously, even if a great distance separates those two particles. The phenomenon also states that two particles in various parts of the universe can mirror the behavior and state of their partner. For particles to be connected across such immeasurable distances, they must send signals to each other that travel faster than the speed of light. Quantum entanglement was once considered impossible, as objects are supposed to be affected by their surroundings, not something happening on the other side of the universe. Quantum entanglement is a bit of an inconvenience as it breaks fundamental laws of classic physics once thought unbreakable. So, what does quantum entanglement prove? When two molecules or particles become entangled, they share momentum, polarization, or spin properties. That being said, if one end moves, there will be a corresponding movement on another end or side. My theory is that your guardian angels are superb in using quantum entanglement or "spooky action at a distance." This could be an aspect of how angels help and guide us here on earth. The angels' actions may be the unexplained movements of vehicles that avoid accidents or the guided directions of bullets that save people's lives. It also explains the strong connections between identical twins and the close bond individuals have to one another.

Angels want you to know they are around you all the time, helping us through our most challenging days as well as to celebrate the good ones. However, praise and worship belong to God. I do believe you can call on your angels for protection, help, and healing as they are sent here for you by God, and of course, you can thank them for the divine intervention.

Thank you, God, for the gift from heaven, a picture of the rainbow eye you sent me and others around the world to witness for themselves, proof of the rainbow portal's existence!

CHAPTER 7

Knowledge

Once I became aware that my dad's spiritual energy would occasionally visit me, I searched for knowledge of how this happens. Back in high school, my sister-in-law, Jenifer, and I took a course on Shaman at The Newman Center Church. It was about mastering altered states of consciousness between the physical and the spiritual world for the sake of obtaining healing and knowledge to help others. I recall the process recommended for meditation, spiritual travel, and things used to guide us. The instructor claimed we each have a Power Animal, and we're supposed to find out what our animal was, however, I couldn't do it. There was an older, wiser man who said he would help me. When he finished his meditation, he said, you have a lot of power animals guiding you! Power animals are defined as guides who may appear in dreams. They are spirit guides who walk through various stages of life with a person, teaching, guiding, and protecting them. This experience reinforced my love of animals and gave me comfort knowing I had this in addition to my many guardian angels helping me through life.

I do not recall when or where, but I received some audiotapes at one point in my teenage years. The concepts in the tapes talked about our ability to travel to other realms for the sake of knowledge through our minds and souls. The idea intrigued me; it made me wonder if the world's geniuses had developed and perfected these skills—karma or the spiritual principle of cause and effect. Good and honorable deeds contribute to good karma, and evil or bad deeds contribute to bad karma.

It further went on to say that if in your life you did not do enough good, you will be reincarnated. Reincarnation was way out of my comfort zone. My path was to be a good person and to be reunited with my parents in heaven when I die. I wanted nothing to do with reincarnation. Who would want to come back to all the pain and suffering people experience here on earth? It seems like it would fit the definition of hell with all the pain and suffering people go through here.

Red Lights

In high school, I had my first astonishing experience of how intuition can help save someone from injury. I was driving home late at night when I approached an intersection. The lights appeared to be flashing yellow, and flashed red in the other direction. I had the right of way to proceed through the intersection as traffic in the opposite directions should have come to a stop. Out of nowhere, I recalled a friend of mine asking me if I knew to stop at flashing red lights as she didn't realize she had to stop. I decided to stop for the flashing yellow lights, just to be safe. As I stopped, a car blew through the intersection. If I had not listened to this inner guidance, I would have been in a serious car crash.

My years of forensic death investigation taught me that T-bone and head-on collisions are statistically the two most deadly car crashes. T-bone collisions are fatal, even at low speeds because of the sudden change in velocity or delta-V. The vehicle going in one direction has a sudden shift in another direction—a change in velocity. This is something that our blood vessels cannot withstand. The consequence is sheering of major blood vessels that results in immediate death from exsanguination. A car also provides less protection from a side impact.

Head-on crashes are so dangerous because the impact's force is doubled by each vehicle's speed in the opposite direction while also looking at the vehicle's center of mass. The calculation of speed—the center of mass with the resulting trajectory or angle of departure is all part of crash reconstruction. Today, more than ever, there are more distracted drivers on the road. When driving on a roadway with oncoming traffic, keeping slightly more right of the centerline is safer while staying in your lane. It may give you the split-second time you need to be able to respond to a fatal head-on collision, as well as listening to your intuition.

A Bultmann Thing

In college, I had the opportunity to take a theology class. The main take-away message for me was that there can be a lot of misinterpretation of what certain things meant thousands of years ago that do not have the same meaning today. Heck, twenty years ago, the pound sign #, was a game of tick tack toe and is now the hashtag #. Just add a couple of thousand years, and one can only begin to imagine what certain words were referencing.

I was able to study the works of a distant relative, Rudolf Bultmann (1884-1976). A German Lutheran theologian and pinnacle figure of liberal Christianity, Bultmann was a professor of the New Testament at the University of Marburg. History and Eschatology (the part of theology concerned with death, judgment, and the soul's final destiny) is one of the densest approaches to understanding history from Christian theology. Eschatology involves four elements or *last* things: death, judgment, heaven, and hell. Bultmann, an exegete, and theologian, instead argued for an existentialist interpretation of the New Testament. Existentialists believe that society should not restrict an individual's life or actions as these restrictions inhibit free will and the development of a person's potential. It evaluates the human experience of faith and how people and cultures express it. Being a theologian is a complex job of conceptualizing and debating the nature of God. The study of theology involves taking on the challenging questions about the meaning of religion.

CHAPTER 8

Grief to Acceptance

I began to understand my journey through grief better once I read the book *The Five Stages of Grief* written by Elisabeth Kubler-Ross. The stages of grief include: denial, anger, bargaining, depression, and acceptance. Each person moves through these stages at various times; some people can also become stuck if they do not work through the stages of grief to acceptance. Grief can also come from many other things. For example, with the worldwide pandemic, you can see many people stuck in the first phase of denial. Denial also includes shock—a state of disbelief and numb feelings.

The first year following a death is by far the hardest. It is not recommended to make big changes in the first year following a significant loss as grief affects the limbic system of the brain. It can throw off how one regulates emotions, concentration, memory, and the ability to multitask. Things get a little easier, but it is never gone; you have to adapt to the change. When you reach acceptance, you begin to realize that their spirit still lives on in your heart as well as around you. Their inner soul angel becomes the fiercest guardian angel watching over us throughout the remainder of our soul's time here on earth.

I was in my early twenties when I decided that I wanted to be a forensic death investigator. I made a conscious decision to turn down my spiritual connection and knowledge of what seemed to be growing stronger. I recall a film about Ouija boards not having the ability to identify the spirit's intent that may be trying to contact you. I wanted no part of anything evil in my life. I had times when I knew my dad was present, but there were other times that I didn't. I did not want anything scary or strange occurring at this point in my life, considering my job. I now know that you should always put God, good intentions, and white light around you to keep you safe as you journey for knowledge with any form of prayer or meditation. I was still early in my learning of truly trusting my intuition. Listening to your intuition may save your life or someone else's life because trusting your intuition is a true gift from God. Now, I know to purely trust it.

Making Murphey a Friend

Murphey's Law is a supposed law of nature. If anything can go wrong, it will. The law is named after Captain Edward A Murphy, an engineer working at Edwards Air force base in 1949. Murphy was working on the Air force project MX981, designed to see how much sudden deceleration a person can stand in a crash. One day he found a transducer wired wrong; he cursed the person responsible, saying, "If there is any way to do it wrong, he'll find it!" The project manager kept a list of laws he now called Murphy's Law. Before this, it was once called Sod's Law. I have a philosophy that Murphey's Law is always ready to spring into action! Therefore, I became friends with Murphy and tried to circumvent his arrival by being ready for him to show up at any given time. Be as prepared as you can. **If you think it, do it!**

Intuitive experiences - Putting it all together

I have chosen to challenge myself by continuing my education and pushing myself to learn new things. This included becoming an RN, followed by a certified registered nurse anesthetist, and now taking on the task of becoming an author.

One day in the OR, the surgeon I was working with pulled some pacemaker wires out of a patient's heart. I told him I would get the crash cart and place it outside the door if we needed it. He immediately cued into what I was feeling and said we should bring the crash cart into the room. The surgery was uneventful as we had thoroughly planned for the worst-case scenario; we planned for Murphy and trusted our intuition. The doctor later told me about a book called *Blink: The Power of Thinking Without Thinking*. It is a fascinating read by Malcolm Gladwell and talked about research from psychology and behavioral economics on the adaptive unconscious as mental processes that work rapidly and automatically from little information. It is when your mind gathers and interprets information faster than your conscious mind can process and communicate it. Gladwell refers to "thin-slicing" as our unconscious to find patterns in situations and behavior based on narrow slices of experience. It is what makes people great at their jobs.

CHAPTER 9

Intuition or Your Guardian Angel?

Avoiding wrong way drivers is a lifesaving message I pass along frequently to people. This principle saved my own life one night in 1995. When driving down a split double-laned highway, I stay in the right lane, especially at night and when rounding curves. Suppose you experience a drunk driver or a confused person who may have entered the highway driving in the wrong direction. The person will be in what they believe is their right lane (slow lane) but in fact, they are in your left lane in the US roadways. This recurrent death scene occurs several times every year. However, it does not cause the most deaths. When you start to see repeat patterns, it is knowledge. Trends and patterns are critical information to follow and help you become great at whatever you choose to do with your life. Once you become an expert at seeing these things, your intuition or that feeling you get tells you how to respond. It may become so great that you react to it before your mind even knows or processes it. In healthcare, it is often this that determines whether you will save a person's life or not.

Approximately 1.35 million people die in traffic crashes each year, or 3,700 people a day. Here are a few other tips. Be cautious when following closely behind trucks that are hauling an open load tied down for an extended period. Many injuries and deaths result from failed safety straps. User error allows items to come loose, impaling vehicles, or rolling off the sides of the trucks resulting in accidents. Try not to pass trucks on the outside lane of significant sharp curves as the center mass of the vehicle or centrifugal force can shift cargo loads causing the truck to tip over. Semi-trucks cause approximately 11 percent of all traffic accident deaths in the U.S. As previously stated, trust your instincts. If you have an uncomfortable feeling when you are driving, perk up and become more aware of your surroundings. It just might be your guardian angel nudging you!

The Angel Who Awakens You!

Dave was a truck driver working for a major trucking business. When he was getting near the end of his run, he felt himself getting tired. He was heading southbound on I-65, approaching the Indianapolis Airport. Dave had fallen asleep behind the wheel, and his truck was veering left when suddenly, he heard a voice yell, "DAVID!" It was the voice of his deceased mother calling his name. He woke abruptly with an adrenaline rush, quickly realized where he was, and noticed his truck had been crossing the lanes of traffic; he was heading for the center median. Dave, thankful no other vehicles were in the left lanes, guided the truck back to the road's right lane. Shaken, he was quickly wide awake and grateful his guardian angel had intervened. Dave shared with me how at the early age of eight, his father had died of a brain hemorrhage, and at the age of twenty-three, he lost his mother to breast cancer. Dave has had several encounters where his mother's spirit would visit him on his travels. She would appear as a glowing sphere of light. He could see her face, but there were no wings. Dave felt like his mother's spirit was there guiding him through tough decisions in his life. A colleague stated that he saw the glow of light illuminating the cab of Dave's truck one night. The light disappeared as the man approached the vehicle. He feels many people have spiritual experiences but are simply afraid to share their stories because of social stigma.

The Life of a Medical Examiner Investigator

My job as a forensic death investigator was fascinating. I loved that every day there was a new story unfolding, and you never knew what the story was going to be. The first six months of any job are challenging just getting used to the process and the people you work with. After, the six-month mark, you get to the cruising speed that is easy to maintain. In this time frame, you can continue to cruise or choose to excel and become an expert at whatever job you do. Being a forensic death investigator was a challenging job, and it took a couple of years to reach a level of expertise. Each death scene was a story left by the deceased, and our job was to figure out or read the story based on the clues they left behind. I loved this aspect of the job and all the other people you met on the scene—police officers, paramedics, water patrol, firefighters, family members, and the news media. The additional perk depended on the scene's location; at times, we were able to offer the deceased one last view of the Minneapolis chain of lakes on the way back to the office. The beautiful views were a method of stress reduction after extremely stressful events.

There is a downside to the job, notifying and talking to the family after a loved one's death. This is one of the most stressful things about the job. However, I chose to view this as one of my unique gifts. I guided families at what is likely a traumatic event in their life while offering them support and direction. It gave me the job satisfaction needed to perform this piece of the job. The smell at times is by far the most unpleasant part of the job but learning to breathe through your mouth is the trick. In addition to washing your hands, face, and nose when you are done. I chuckle when people say to put something like Vick's vapor rub under your nose. Now you are just breathing in through your nose more, and it makes your nose run! The last thing you want to be doing in these conditions is having your nose dripping and touching your face. Thankfully Covid 19 taught most people this aspect of hygiene and the importance of washing your hands. The one nice part of wearing a mask is placing a scent inside the mask versus your face, or chewing gum also works to cover up odors.

What makes or breaks any job you do is the people you work with. I have had the pleasure to work with so many brilliant and talented people throughout my life. I have been very blessed in that way. I have tried to stay open to receiving knowledge from people who have come into my life so that they might share their stories with me. Coming across as arrogant does not make someone want to teach you the tricks of the trade. Although this can sometimes be hard, especially if their vibrational frequency is very different from yours, it is still best to stay humble and kind.

I have many fond memories of working the weekend shifts with Linda and Paul at the Hennepin County Medical Examiner's office. We incorporated laughter and joy into everything we did. One day Linda and I were both working the day shift. A maintenance worker came out of the autopsy suite and asked me where to put the 400-pound autopsy table that he had just replaced with a new one. I looked around our hallways, where there wasn't much room to begin with, when my eyes locked on the investigator manager's office across the hallway. It was long and narrow, the perfect spot to store this table.

Come on, Linda, we can help these guys lift this 400-pound table through that narrow door frame. It was times like this my powerlifting came in very handy! We did it! We put the long silver heavy metal table right in the middle of his office. We waited with eager anticipation of our manager Mike's return. Mike had gray hair, usually dressed in a suit, and wore a trench coat. I heard the stairwell door closing, and the sound of his dress shoes echoed in the hallway as he approached his office. He stopped dead in his tracks as his eyes met the heavy metal cold table sitting in the middle of his office. The stature of his body and chest stiffened as the words came flying out of his mouth. WTF!

If there is one thing I have learned in this life, don't lie. It is far better to suffer the consequences of what happened with the truth than to suffer the effects of the lie. Lies will not only trip you up, but the stress of lying can have health consequences on your body. The list includes heart attacks, strokes, and alopecia, to name a few.

I owned it right away. I walked out of our small office where three investigators work. I began explaining to Mike how the maintenance worker had nowhere to put the table where it wouldn't be in the way of day-to-day operations. I said your office seemed like the best place for it. This way, when you call us into your office, you can ask us to lie down as I laughed. I didn't get in trouble since I owned it and told the truth. The table ended up staying in his office for several weeks. It made all of us laugh when we could hear him grumbling about the table from across the hallway. Laughter is the best medicine.

Making the List

Training of new investigative staff included having them observe an autopsy. Lynne, one of my female colleagues, attended an autopsy of a homicide victim and the process. The homicide detectives and officers who processed the scene also came to the autopsy to have multiple sources of the findings and take pictures of all the evidence. On this day, Lynne had the opportunity to visit with a charming detective. Lynne snuck out of the autopsy suite to come and tell me. You need to meet this guy! He has a lot going for him, and not to mention, he is cute. Lynne already had a life partner, so I appreciated that she was looking out for me. I told her I was not meeting anyone over a dead body, but I was willing to come and take a look. I opened the door, and I agreed with her assessment. I made a mental note of the name and wondered if I would run into him at a scene in the future. It was interesting how his name was in the paper for solving a cold case murder attempt the following week. The story was a horrific one. A male came to the door of an elderly female and shot her in the face so that he could take her television to his college dorm. I was highly impressed he took the time to track a cold case, finding justice for the elderly woman and her family. This was the talk of our office, and I further learned he was in a master's class with my manager. BOOM! not only did he make it on my list, but he also rose to the top of it! I will keep an eye out for this guy.

Following Intuition

I recall going to a death scene across the street from First Avenue in Minneapolis, MN, a live music venue made famous by Prince. In the early 1990s, there was a homeless shelter across the street. We went to death scenes in pairs, and my partner at the time was the one writing the case and I was taking pictures and would get the cot and stretcher. As I was heading down the flight of stairs to retrieve the cot, a large man working at the shelter asked me if I needed any help. Usually, I would say no as the stretcher wasn't heavy, but this time I had a powerful and uncomfortable feeling come over me. I listened to the awkward feeling, and I thanked him for helping me. He went down the final flight of stairs with me and just as I opened the door to head over to the medical examiner's suburban, a man walking on the street started running toward me, yelling, "I am going to fucking kill you!" The large man intervened and saved me from physical harm as he tackled the stranger before he could get to me. I was shaken, but so thankful that I followed my intuition and my guardian angels for having him there to protect me.

Paying attention to your intuition or the feeling you receive is a form of protection from God and a way of protecting yourself. Suppose your messages are to hurt yourself or to hurt someone else. These messages are NOT coming from GOD. I would recommend you receive help from a medical professional or your spiritual leader, church, pastor, or priest if the message is to harm other people. God wants to help you find peace. Peace can be found by letting go of past negativity and acknowledge past karma, releasing it, and then moving on to live your life in the present and not allowing the past to ruin your future.

The Inner Soul Angels Release

After thousands of death scenes, I began to realize that most of the souls or spirits were already gone by the time we arrived to perform the scene investigation. The energy or feeling I would get when one was around was not there, at least not in the sense that it would bring chills followed by an adrenaline response that would occur if a spirit were prominently still around. I only had a few experiences where the energy of the spirit had remained prominent, after having thousands of occasions where the soul's energy was gone from the physical body. My personal experiences told me this was vastly different from what I was taught. The soul and the body will come back to life on the last day. Those writings seem more like the zombie apocalypse. Dogma, in a broad sense, is any belief held unquestioningly and with undefended certainty. I realized that some of the writings were manufactured to instill fear, guilt, and obedience. I knew many things were not correct, but I was not at a point in my life to search for the truth.

My quest made me continue to ponder the length of time the portal to heaven is open. For some, it is available for shorter periods, while for others it appears to be open longer. If the spirit, for some reason, does not want to leave or does not leave in time, it can get stuck on an earthly spiritual plane.

Crime Scene Guidance

During a homicide investigation, the medical investigator's office works very closely with law enforcement. Homicide Detectives at the homicide scene also come for the autopsy as part of the investigation of documenting evidence. In Minneapolis, MN, if the murder occurred there, we would have a Minneapolis homicide detective and Bureau of Investigations (B of I) personnel come over for the autopsy. If the death were in Hennepin County, the Hennepin County Crime Lab Investigator would come over for the autopsy. Unlike TV programs where one person is the superhero who does it all, several people work as a team to process a death investigation scene and put all the pieces together in real life. I asked a former colleague who had worked at the Hennepin County Sheriff's Crime Lab back when I worked at the medical examiner's office his opinion on some things I was writing in my book about clocks and time because he fixes clocks in his spare time. He shared a similar story about knowledge coming to him through a dream that helped him solve a murder. He had a homicide case of a woman who was found floating in a transparent plastic bag wrapped with a cord. The body was found in the water near Theodore Wirth Park in Golden Valley, MN. He had been at the autopsy that day and would have processed all the evidence along with the medical examiner's office staff. That night, he dreamed of the deceased female figure walking towards him with her hands out. In the figure's hands was a phone cord with glowing green specs covering the cable. The following day he called down to the medical examiner's office to reexamine the cord that bound the female's body once he woke up. As he reexamined the cord, he saw it was flat like a kind of phone cord which would have been stapled to the wall; as he looked closer at the cord, ever so tiny green specs of paint were on the cord! The same specs that were glowing in his dream. A search warrant was obtained for the murder victim's boyfriend's residence. They found a new phone cord wrapper in the garbage and a new phone cord that had been stapled back onto the wall. The tiny green specs matched the paint color of the walls in the apartment. This man was later arrested for the murder of his girlfriend. Her spirit was stuck until she could give this piece of knowledge, now her inner soul angel was free to move on to the heavenly plane.

STELLA Is That You?

It was a beautiful Minnesota summer day when I received a call from a Minneapolis police officer requesting an investigator to the scene of a deceased female in Minneapolis on Blaisdell Ave S. Linda and I headed out to the scene. At the same time, Joe stayed back at the office to complete the other reports. Upon entering the house's front door, an antique desk with a reading light was immediately to the left. One of the officers was sitting at the desk writing his report. I took a glance around the room. To the right was a stairway leading up to the bedrooms. Straight in front of me was the strangest picture hanging on the wall. The picture had a dual image; it was a beautiful lady looking in the mirror and a very prominent skull. The picture is called *All is Vanity*. I thought it was extremely odd to put this type of picture right at the front entrance, so it would be one of the first things one would see when entering the home.

I stopped briefly to get a report from the officer sitting at the desk. He gave me the deceased name and date of birth. We will call her Stella for this story as I wish the dead to rest in peace. Stella did not have family in the area, and neighbors had called to check on her welfare. "Looks like a natural death," the officer replied. The officer had interviewed several neighbors prior to our arrival. He hadn't been able to locate a set of keys to lock up the house yet. An attorney was handling her trust and was a friend of one of her neighbors. The officer related that some neighbors stated Stella didn't like that neighbor, but he asked for the house's keys when we leave. I informed the officer that once we locate the house's keys, we would lock it up and turn over the property to the family once they are notified.

The officer said Stella was upstairs and led me to the back bedroom. I was standing in the doorway; a long dresser was straight ahead of me against the left wall. Off to the right, but in the center of the room, was a queen-sized bed with a large brass headboard and a slightly smaller footboard. The two windows were each covered with a dark red velvet drapery that went all the way to the floor. The two pieces were cinched closed with a decorative metal clasp. Stella was on the floor lying on her back at the foot end of the bed, in the space between the bed and the dresser. Her feet were toward the bedroom door, and her head was slightly under the brass rail. She was dressed in her nightgown. All the top covers were down on the ground next to her; only a fitted sheet remained on the bed. Stella's cane was in the center of the bed. I examined Stella's tiny, malnourished body and the bedroom. I agreed with the officer; it looked like a natural death.

I moved inside the room, now standing next to the bed facing the doorway where the officer stood, while Linda was next to the dresser to get the body carrier and body bag ready. I was writing the scene and body description when I was suddenly hit in the back just below my left scapula. I turned around quickly to see nothing behind me but the cane lying on the bed. WTF! My stomach dropped; the feeling was beyond simple chills. This was an uncomfortable feeling where the hair stood up on my skin. It was more of a painful prickly feeling at this time and different than anything I had ever felt before. The fight and flight response kicked in, and I was leaving! I told Linda, let's get Stella wrapped up and get out of here. We brought her out to the tan Suburban truck and loaded her in.

I told Linda what had just happened in the room. I could still feel the sting on my back where I had been hit. Oh shit, we still needed to find keys to lock up the house. We were going to have to go back inside. The officers were looking for keys on the main floor. Linda and I were headed back upstairs to check the second bedroom. This time I was now invading Linda's personal space as we ascended the stairs together. We searched the other bedroom and had no keys. Downstairs we went. I proceeded through the small living room dining room area to the kitchen. I was walking towards one of the officers in the kitchen when a free-standing oscillating fan crashed to the ground between us. I turned around quickly, scanning the room. My eyes locked on the area above the kitchen sink, where a large magnet strip had been attached to the wall. Every sized knife a person would want was stuck to that magnet. I heard an officer call from the dining room that he had found the keys! Thank God as I darted out of the kitchen before any of those knives started moving! The officer shut off all the lights and locked the door behind us. He handed me the keys, placing them into a property inventory envelope. Linda and I were in the Suburban when Hennepin County dispatch told us we had another scene to go to. I was relieved to be out of there, and Linda would be writing the next case.

I had been on hundreds of death scenes, and souls had all traveled on, but this scene was different. Was Stella trying to tell me something? We completed the next scene and proceeded back to the office. Finally starting to calm down, we took the elevator down to the lower level. The lower level contained the body processing room, cooler, autopsy suite, and investigative offices. I went into the cooler to grab a large metal cart to place Stella's body on. The top-heavy metal tray is removable; a built-in handle is on each end, and all four sides have a three-to four-inch-high metal edge. The cart holding the tray is equally sturdy and has sizeable thick metal prongs holding the metal tray in place. We transferred her tiny body over to the tray when suddenly the heavy metal tray came up and out the progs hitting me at the top of my pelvis. This was not an expected result for a tray to slide. Stella's spirit was here!

I proceeded to tell the story of what happened to Joe and Mel, the autopsy technician. Joe liked to give everyone a good deal of ribbing and proceeded to give me a hard time about what had happened. My reply was simply if I die before you, I will whack you with a cane or something to let you know it is real. We laughed. Mel left to process the body after hearing the story. It wasn't two minutes later that Mel ran back into the office asking, we aren't autopsying her, are we? I replied, hell no! The blade would probably come off the saw. I asked why what happened. Mel, now visibly disturbed, said, I was pushing the metal cart into the processing room when the coffee can where we placed all the soda pop tops for charity flew across the room, spilling all the tops all over the room. Holy Shit! I couldn't wait to finish writing my case and leave work.

I went to the gym before going home that night to my one-bedroom apartment. That night I went to pull my blinds shut when three plants on a corner stand about a foot away from where I was tipped over, spilling all the plants and dirt on the ground. I began to wonder what Stella wanted and did something happen to her that she was trying to communicate to me.

I thought back to when my job role had switched from being an investigative assistant to an investigator. Now I could write homicide cases. I was outside a house in Minneapolis where the man was slumped over in the bushes next to the front steps. The officer stated the Minneapolis homicide unit was out but did not think it was a homicide. The deceased didn't live at the house, likely someone struggling with chemical dependency. I went up to the deceased and saw a tear in his blue jeans on the right back pocket. I put a pair of gloves on and proceeded to feel his head. It didn't feel right to me, and my intuition told me this man was murdered. I told the officer to call the Minneapolis homicide detective back to the scene. I could see the irritation on his face, but the Medical Examiner has jurisdiction over a death scene. We were going to be processing the scene as a homicide. I called our on-call forensic pathologist to come to the location. I explained the situation and the differing points of view. We processed everything like a homicide. The deceased hands get papers bags taped around them, and the body bag would be sealed with a locking tag. The bag is not opened until everyone is together for the autopsy. The autopsy revealed blunt force injury to the man's head; it was a homicide. I received a lot of congratulations on my first official homicide case as I was the only one who thought it was a homicide, and I listened to my intuition.

The following day, I entered our case review, where I shared Stella's bizarre set of circumstances with the staff and the forensic pathologist. I asked if we could please x-ray her head to ensure we aren't missing something. I was referring to what the officer stated that Stella did not like the man next door and the eagerness of wanting Stella's house keys. The chief medical examiner said, let's do an autopsy and make sure everything is ok. Later that morning, I was headed out to another scene when I saw Mel in the room with Stella. He shot me a very concerned look, and I whispered, I am sorry! When we got back from the scene, the initial autopsy results were in, and the case remained natural as I had initially written it. A short time later, Mike took a call from one of Stella's neighbors, reporting all the lights were back on in her house.

I was puzzled about what Stella was trying to communicate. I thought the only thing left was the neighbor and his connection to her attorney. Being out of any other ideas, I made the strangest call to a family I had ever made. Stella had a sister who lived out of town. I informed her of the natural death and autopsy results. I told her there had been some very odd things going on, and I wondered if Stella was trying to let us know to be cautious of her neighbor's intentions. Stella's sister replied in the sweetest voice. Honey, I am 86 years old, and I cannot come there, but I will send my daughter, and I will tell her everything you have told me. I gave her my sympathy before ending the call. Later that day, the funeral home came and picked up Stella's body. I told Stella I had done everything I could for you. It was time for you to go. Stella left that day, and nothing else occurred after this. I believe Stella wanted me to make sure her sister knew about the neighbor.

On the weekends when Linda, Paul, and I would work together. There were always a lot of noises that would occur here with the air drafts connected to the hospital's tunnels. We would be sitting in the office, and something would fall out in the hall. Then I would hear Paul say, in his old lady voice, "Stella is that you?" We would all laugh, breaking the uneasiness we felt from the unknown.

CHAPTER 10

Spirits Who Make an Appearance

After many years of forensic death investigation, I realized I needed a change. I went back to school to become a nurse, while continuing part time as an investigator, with the intention of one day becoming a certified registered nurse anesthetist. It was during my years of nursing that spirits began to show their abilities. I was amazed by the number of stories and times spirits presented themselves in the community hospitals I worked. The visiting spiritual realm can control lights and electrical things with their energy. It is by far the most common experience I have had. Dim lights will suddenly brighten, or lights will turn on or suddenly go off. While working in the ICU at night, a cardiac monitor went off when there was no patient in that room. There was electrical energy in the room and the monitors were picking it up! I once walked by the monitors for viewing x-rays, and it illuminated, even though it required a flip switch to turn it on. It is a straightforward way for a spirit to get your attention.

Over these six years, my beliefs on how spirits have the energy to influence electrical items was repeatedly validated on the night shift. My colleague, Jill, and I occasionally talked about the things that occurred. There was one room in particular where patients would complain about strange occurrences. One man put on his call light, wondering why people would be working on the building and talking in the middle of the night while he was trying to sleep. Jill told me several years after I left that there was a young man who spent an extended period in that room fighting for his life. Several older patients who stayed in the room made comments to the staff. One older lady told the nurse she needed to remove the young man standing in her room. Jill could not see him, but the patient could. Another older man asked Jill during her rounds if that young man ever found his family. Jill knew who they were talking about and felt terrible that his spirit had remained at the hospital.

For me, other than being aware of their presence, I tried not to engage. I did, however, have one reoccurring experience that I became fond of, and it made me smile. This particular event only happened at night. I would be walking alone down the hall to catch the elevator up to the ICU to start the night shift. As I approached the elevator, the doors would mysteriously open. There were no sensors at this time, and I had not pushed the button. There was never anyone on the elevator when it opened. It gave me a creepy feeling the first couple of times this happened because it just opened. I took this as a gesture of kindness. One day I finally shared this experience with another colleague, Paul, who worked there for many years. Once I shared it, it never happened again, so the spirit seemed content with me being aware of their existence. Newer facilities may have light sensors that turn the lights on when you walk by or go into a room. The experiences I am talking about occurred with old flip switches and dimmer switches long before sensors. Paul also had many recurrent stories at this hospital. The one that occurred the most for him was when he would leave a room and switch off the lights in the morgue. Upon returning after a brief period, all the lights were back on, but no one else was working in there at the time.

Spiritual Travel

At this hospital, I began to have more experiences with patients having spiritual travel and showing signs that the angels were coming. One night I heard the cardiac monitor alarm. I looked at the monitor to see my patient no longer had a cardiac rhythm; he was asystole or flat line. I ran to the room and slid the glass door and curtain open. I quickly asked him if he was all right as I headed for the room lights. I suddenly heard the man say, "I just had the craziest dream! I was out in the hallway, and I saw a huge fellow in the next room." As the man talked, I looked at the EKG monitor in his room as the flat line returned to a normal sinus rhythm. My body was full of adrenaline as I was getting ready to initiate a code blue call. I talked with the patient, who told me stories about being a WWII veteran. After confirming he was doing well, I closed the curtain and glass doors as sound barriers. I walked a few doors down to see another RN, Dale, who recently received a new patient admission. To my shock, the patient was an unkept obese male who Dale was grumbling about how he was going to get the patient clean. My jaw must have hit the floor when I saw the man; my patient had just described from his bed a few doors down.

Reaching for Heaven

It was another busy day shift when I recall receiving a patient back to the ICU whose oxygen saturation dropped. I was in the room tending to the patient when I saw him reaching his hands up into the air above him. I immediately knew what was happening; the angels were there to take him. I said, "Not today," as I hit the code blue button and started to assist the man's breathing. A team arrived to intubate the patient. The angels did not take him that day, but they were there. Reaching up in the air is common when someone is near death when the inner soul angel is set to leave the body.

Listen

I know the importance of listening more to what a patient is feeling or trying to explain. At times this can be challenging based on their medical experience or understanding of medical terminology to explain things to you. It's the same way the spiritual world communicates. How you receive the communication may be different from how someone else understands it, and there will always be people who will never hear or see the message. No proof will ever be enough. Some have eyes but cannot see. I remember one evening when I was working as an intensive care nurse, I had to travel to another floor because of a staffing issue. I was caring for an older lady who told me she knew there was something more that was wrong with her; she had a feeling of impending doom. I called the physician to see if he could see her. I had just helped her into bed when I realized she wasn't breathing. I hit the code blue button The patient quickly regained a level of semiconsciousness after assisting her breathing with an Ambu-bag before the doctor decided to move her to the ICU. I was happy to follow her back to the ICU to take care of her. As we moved this patient into the ICU, I remember the clock flying off the wall as we brought her into the room. I thought her guardian angels were here with her as well as the team working to save her life. The group stayed focused on the task at hand, saving the patient who had gone into acute renal failure! The doctor placed a central venous catheter in her internal jugular vein. The patient later received dialysis and survived.

When Things go Awry

Several of my colleagues were in the breakroom when a pile of papers went flying off the counter. The nurse said, "Okay, now who is on comfort care?" The nurses knew when the spirits were coming for someone. Spirits can be mischievous!

It is impressive how many hospitals have a lot of unexplained issues with medical equipment not working, then working again. Numerous staff members over the years have questioned the possibility of a mischievous spirit being the issue. It would be a fascinating study for a hospital with these problems to have an authentic medium come in to help guide the wandering lost spirit or stuck souls to cross over and find the portal to heaven. The report would be fascinating, not to mention what it would do for the souls to finally be free.

CHAPTER 11

Angels Save Lives

There are times in life when a person's guardian angel can be vividly noted. One of the most common stories I hear from other people regarding angels saving their lives involves motor vehicle accidents or close calls with vehicles, and the angel's ability to provide a force of protection.

The Anchor

Traci had just finished dropping off her two beautiful grandbabies at their aunt's house after spending the weekend together. Traci gracefully hopped back into her sporty black Mustang. She was driving Westbound on Highway 10 at sixty-five miles an hour through congested, heavy lake traffic when the cars in front of her came to a screeching halt. She slammed on the brakes, narrowly missing the car in front of her. Behind her, a truck pulling a boat began breaking hard; there was not enough distance to stop as he plowed into the back of her beautiful Mustang. Behind the truck and boat was another truck. The second truck also crashed into the boat, causing the boat to fly up over the owner's truck. A cinder block, which was used as an impromptu boat anchor, continued to project forward, turning into a launched missile. It smashed out the back window of Traci's Mustang; the rear seat where her granddaughters had been sitting just ten minutes before. What happened next is miraculous, as the cinder block should have continued straight through the car, hitting Traci in the back of the head. According to Newton's first law of motion, a body in motion at a constant velocity will remain in motion in a straight line unless acted upon by an outside force. Instead, the cinder block, bounced up out of the broken back window, flying up over the car, and smashing the front window before coming to rest on the dash in front of the steering wheel where Traci was driving. Witnesses to the accident immediately told Traci her guardian angel was watching over her! There was a higher, more powerful force protecting Traci that day.

A Beautiful Bike Ride

In July of 2018, I met Elizabeth while attending a concert with some mutual friends. Elizabeth mentioned she was continuing to recover from an accident two years earlier. Elizabeth had gone out for a bike ride on a beautiful summer day near her home when she noticed a van driving at a high speed. She immediately had the feeling she should move off the roadway to a safer area. Pulling off the road, Elizabeth remembered looking up at the sky and saying, "Thank you, God, for a beautiful day." The van passed her safely but concealed behind the van was a Ford F150 truck barreling straight toward her. Elizabeth was struck from behind by the Ford F150 truck. She recalls everything turning white while being sprawled out like a snow angel. She recounts floating in a place of timelessness when she saw the tan hands of a man slowly bringing her down to the ground millimeters at a time. The white began to fade away, and the sky turned blue again. She was now sitting on the ground in the most proper sitting position, holding onto her left leg. She looked up to see hundreds of white angels moving frantically, buzzing around a two-foot radius, working on healing her body. Her left leg was completely broken at a ninety-degree angle. The truck left the accident scene. Elizabeth said to the unknown driver, "I forgive you." A young man in the van came back to help her. She asked him if he hit her, to which he replied, "No." The helicopter air ambulance arrived to give her emergency care and a quick ride to North Memorial Trauma Center in Robbinsdale, MN. As she was rushed into the stabilization room, the lights became blindingly bright; she could barely keep her eyes open. She grabbed her sunglasses from a pouch on the back of her jersey. As she put on her sunglasses, she said, "Okay, now I'm ready," and held out her arms as they worked quickly to cut away her clothing. She said, "The only things wrong with me are my broken left ankle and right knee." She was bloody, bruised, and had road rash all over. The doctors sent her off to the CT scanner to confirm no other life-threatening injuries. She was right! Elizabeth said the bike helmet helped save her life from more severe injuries when her head hit the truck's windshield. Her back had broken off the side mirror of the Ford F150 as she came down off the top of the truck. The broken mirror was the evidence the authorities eventually used to identify the man who had left the accident scene. The bike ended up wrapped in a barbed-wire fence, and her left shoe was never found at the scene.

God's angels saved Elizabeth's life that day. She was still needed here on earth to be there for her beautiful children and share this miraculous story with all of us. Thank you for the Power Angel's ability to wrap their wings around a person to protect them from harm.

Spooky Action at a Distance

My husband and I were on our way to my family's home for Christmas. We reached the area around Fergus Falls near a wayside rest area. In this location, the westbound lanes are significantly elevated over the eastbound lanes, and a steep center hill serves as a median between the two roadways. We saw the car in front of us starting to lose control as the entire highway was covered in black ice. My husband let his foot off the gas as we began to hit the ice, but we slid sideways on the road straight towards the steep embankment. The unfortunate side of death investigation is sometimes seeing the accident playing out in your mind. I knew if we went over the embankment; it would have been a front, end over end, rollover. A bad reaction on my part—I brought my feet up onto the dash to brace myself for impact. In hindsight, if the airbags deployed, they would have broken my legs and pelvis. Airbags deploy at speeds of 200 miles an hour, then quickly deflate so not to impair vision and body movements. It all happens in about 0.25 of a second.

The two front wheels of our car hit the edge of the embankment, turning us ninety degrees and directed us back in the direction we were once traveling. It was like something had just lifted the truck and put us back on the road in the correct direction! It was both miraculous and scary at the same time. We thanked our guardian angels for keeping us safe from harm. It was not until meeting my friend Jason in the August of 2021 that I understood how this could be an example of quantum entanglement or spooky action at a distance. Thank you, Jason, for sharing your knowledge of quantum entanglement with me!

Guardian Angels in Action

On the evening of Tuesday, September 25, 2018, Lori was on her way home from the gym. She was driving alone in her new white Chevy Transverse, heading eastbound on County Road 9, driving at sixty to sixty-five miles an hour. Lori knew 120 Street intersected County Road 9 from the right; no roadway was on the left, just a field with trees. Lori had the right of way, while 120 Street had a stop sign. It was dark outside as she saw headlights quickly approaching from 120 Street causing Lori's instincts to kick in. The vehicle was not slowing down enough to stop at the stop sign. Lori had already begun slowing down to about forty-five miles an hour when she hit the brakes. The black full-size SUV, traveling around sixty had not even slowed down for the stop sign. Initially, Lori closed her eyes at the point of impact, but then she opened them as she saw everything in slow motion. She felt like she had time to think. According to Lori, the vehicle seemed illuminated, and she had a warm feeling like she was going to be okay. "Let the wheel go." As she listened and let go of the wheel, she watched the airbags deploy and watched the horizon along with other car lights spin. The vehicle finally came to rest in a field on the northside of County Road 9. Her vehicle was now underneath a tree facing the road. She looked around to see if a door was open as she thought it might be where the light was coming from. No doors were open, and the light was no longer on. Getting out, she realized how lucky she was; the vehicle ended up inches away from a green electrical post and a tree, but she didn't hit a single thing in the field. She walked away from the accident with a nondisplaced left wrist fracture and pain in her left knee. The other vehicle flipped onto the driver's side with the headlights facing east, the vehicle came to rest seven trees deep into the field but did not strike a single tree. The other driver was in his forties. He was alone in the vehicle and suffered no significant injuries. Fortunately, he was able to crawl out of his vehicle's passenger window. Lori recalled seeing two small car seats in the back of the black SUV. The officer said the man had left his home after arguing with his wife. She didn't know if he thought he was on a different road since there was no roadway on the other side of the stop sign. I found the story and timing to be nothing short of a miracle. Lori struck the black SUV in the rear quarter panel of the driver's side. The vehicle's momentum and resulting post-crash trajectory caused the black SUV to spin and safely come to rest in a field. If Lori had not slowed down in anticipation, the point of impact would have been in the SUV's driver's door resulting in death or severe injury to the driver. Yet if Lori had been able to come to a complete stop, the SUV would have continued further into the field and stand of trees, resulting in catastrophic results for the other driver. Thank you, God, for sending the angels to protect Lori and the other driver.

CHAPTER 12

Angels at Work

On February 2, 2019, I cared for Eric, who was newly diagnosed with lymphoma and required a port placement for chemotherapy. I asked Eric how he discovered the lymphoma at the early age of thirty-five. Eric revealed he had picked up a side job for a friend who had injured himself. The job required Eric to do some heavy lifting. Eric felt like there was something wrong after he finished working. He was not sure if he had appendicitis or what the problem was. He went to the emergency department for evaluation and a CT showed lymphoma. I told Eric how his guardian angels were watching over him to have found this as early and as quickly as it was.

In a conversation about guardian angels, Eric told me about his son Connor. Eric said when Connor was less than two years old, he was admitted to the emergency room. On January 28, 2016, he had a fast-growing abscess on the right side of his neck near the back of his throat. Connor needed to be intubated and quickly transferred by helicopter to the children's hospital because his airway was starting to close. This story was remarkably familiar to me. I told Eric I remember intubating his son in the ER. Knowing this child was going to be intubated for an extended period, I told the doctor I wanted to get a micro-cuffed endotracheal tube. Before my employment, the hospital did not carry micro-cuffed endotracheal tubes, so they were not readily available. I had ordered them because they help prevent subglottic stenosis, which is damage to the pediatric airway, especially for those who needed to be intubated for an extended period. I went back to the OR, grabbing my emergency equipment bag, which I had stocked for just this type of emergency. The ER physician and I orchestrated an emergency rapid sequence induction which put Connor asleep. I used a video laryngoscope camera called a GlideScope to see Connor's vocal cords. The tool allows the doctor the same view I had in case I needed any assistance with the intubation, as in this situation, the airway can swell immediately. I secured the endotracheal tube tightly with tape as I knew this was Connor's lifeline until IV antibiotics could reduce the infection and swelling in his throat. Connor was now asleep when the helicopter staff arrived to take Connor and transfer him down to the children's hospital. Eric confirmed that he also recalled me leaving to get a different tube to prevent damage. I told Eric that I had something for him. I excused myself and went to my locker to get an angel coin for Eric. I wear an angel wing necklace in the wintertime since my mother's death. It displays acknowledgment of angels' existence in our lives. I needed all the protection I could get, and Eric now needed extra protection too. Upon returning to the preoperative room, I gave Eric the angel coin to remind him that in the tough times there is always something far greater watching over us!

During the time I was away getting the angel coin, Eric called his wife, Jackie, and told her the story of meeting me. Eric told me Jackie remembered me taking care of their son, Connor.

Eric told me the rest of Connor's story. I wouldn't believe that Connor was now five! Whenever Connor sees a helicopter in the area, he says, "Daddy, my angels that came to save me!" I was flooded with emotion, pride, and joy knowing that I was a team member who participated in this happy and successful outcome for Connor's story. The last thing I heard about Connor several years before was that somehow the endotracheal tube had become dislodged and required replacement. They struggled with the ability to get a new ET tube back in Connor due to the swelling.

I took care of Eric for his port placement and told his nurse in the recovery area this fantastic story. Pam smiled in awe, then told me how Eric is the Godfather to her son, Arik. How ironic is that! After checking with the hospital's patient privacy on how to go about sharing the story, they informed me that if the patient is willing to share information, it would be allowed. Thanks to the nurse, I knew I would be able to check in on Eric's progress and one day get their permission to share this incredible story.

Two years later, on January 27, 2021, I called Jackie and Eric to follow up on their progress and accurately describe what happened. They both permitted me to share their story for this book. Jackie was emotional as the following day was the five-year anniversary of Conner's trip to the ER. Jackie told me her grandpa had died just three weeks before. Everyone in their family had been sick following his death. Connor was twenty-one months at the time and was not talking well enough to tell them what was wrong. Jackie dropped off their other children and proceeded to the ER when she noticed a small hard bump on the side of Connors's neck. The doctor wanted Connor to have a CT scan. He told her he was going to send Connor by ambulance to the children's hospital. Eric was able to make it to the ER by the time the results of the CT scan were finished. It revealed a growing abscess at the back of the throat. The condition was elevated to a genuine emergency. The helicopter and the anesthesia department were called. Jackie said the abscess ended up being a staphylococcus (staph) infection requiring antibiotics.

In the children's hospital, Connor remained heavily sedated while on the ventilator and waiting for the antibiotics to treat the infection. One day the staff were attempting to wean the sedation, and as they did, Connor woke up enough to get a hold of his endotracheal tube. Jackie and Eric do not know what happened, but he was not getting enough oxygen, his heart rate had dropped, causing a code blue. Jackie remembered feeling her grandpa's presence and knew he was there watching over Connor. I asked if Connor remembers anything from the past now that he is older. Eric and Jackie said he doesn't talk much about it anymore, but they had kept a scrapbook of when Connor was in the hospital, and he is aware he almost died. I asked Eric how the treatment for the lymphoma was going. He had about four months of treatment left. Today he is feeling great and in remission. Eric remarked Follicular Lymphoma is extremely rare, especially to have found it in someone so young.

Eric said it was the strangest thing. Just the other week, he opened a drawer that contained the piece of paper with my name on it. He was wondering if I was going to call him about their story. I then explained some details of how my experiences had turned from just writing about their story into drafting an entire book about angels. Connor's story is a classic example of why you might be in a particular place at a specific time to do a job and order the right supplies. This was my case with Connor. I remember having a powerful sense that I needed to update the pediatric supplies and update this hospital with emergency response equipment. I recall stating if it saved even one life, it would be worth it, and it was all worth it!

Thank you, Eric, Jackie, and Connor, for letting me share your story of angels at work. May God and the angels continue to bless and protect you.

CHAPTER 13

Perspective

The attitude and response to situations affect the body's health through its physiological responses. Put simply, having a positive perspective will improve health. The law of attraction suggests that positive thoughts bring positive results into a person's life, while negative thoughts bring adverse outcomes. Magnetism is a physical phenomenon produced by the motion of electric charge, resulting in attractive and repulsive forces between objects.

Applying the positive law of attraction and daily gratitude can help give a purposeful perspective to deal with memories of difficult situations. Mental toughness is not always easy. It takes a lot of practice and a lot of willpower at times to stay the course. Things that may help include spending peaceful quality time in nature, exercise, contemplation, hobbies, and crafts as a great way to increase your body's endorphins. Spending time away from the ever-constant barrage of electronic overload that is decaying the mind as well as the connection to your intuition can help restore peace.

The National Institute of Health (NIH) indicates children who spend more than two hours a day on screen time score lower on language and thinking tests. More than seven hours a day of screen time thins the brain's cortex— the area of the brain related to critical thinking and reasoning.

A Positive Perspective

I have met several people who have viewed their illness or injury as a blessing in their life because of a strange set of circumstances that revealed the underlying problem and saved their life. One gentleman I met had bumped his head while working out in his garage. A lingering headache remained so he decided to seek medical care. The physician ordered a CT scan of the man's head, and while there was no severe bleeding from the trauma, it did show a small brain tumor growing, and surgery was quickly scheduled to remove the mass. Although this was a terrifying time in his life, and filled with many uncertainties, the man's positive perspective helped him find comfort by looking at the event to be a blessing that saved his life. The tumor was removed successfully, and he has been healthy ever since.

Having negative attitudes creates chronic stress, which changes the body's hormone balance, resulting in physiological changes. It depletes the chemicals within the brain required for happiness and further damages the immune system.

Sounds No One Else Can Hear

A bizarre story, which became a huge blessing, was the story of a small group of people having an odd conversation about hearing things that you do not share with other people. One of the ladies in the group said, "Oh, you mean like hearing crying babies?" In the group was a neurosurgeon who instantly tuned in to what the woman was saying. He immediately ordered a CT scan of her brain, discovering she had a berry aneurysm. It is the most common type of intracranial aneurysm. An aneurysm is a bulge or ballooning from a weakened area in the wall of a blood vessel. People with a brain aneurysm may hear sounds that are not heard by others. Sometimes it can even sound like explosions. Fortunately, the surgical repair of her aneurysm was a success. The irony of this conversation occurring when it did was the true blessing that saved her life. If you have this type of symptom, see your doctor immediately.

68

The Present

At times, terrible things do happen to good people. When our soul's mission here on earth is over, it does not matter where you are, or how old you are—your inner soul angel will transform, leaving the human body behind. The guardian angels will be there with your inner soul angel, guiding you home.

Is there something within your own life you could attempt to give a positive perspective? Forgiving and releasing negative moments, along with the negative energy it attracts so your heart and soul can be free. The release will give you a brighter future, free from a clouded past. All that is guaranteed in life is right now! Having an appreciation and being grateful for all the little blessings and living each day in the present.

CHAPTER 14

Little Signs an Angel May Be Near

Each person will be different in what kinds of signs they may receive, while others may feel frustrated by the signs not being significant to allow them to realize it is a sign. Some people may feel the energy around them, smell a particular scent, perfume, cologne, smoke, or some may see glimpses of light or orbs while a small fraction can see the spirit. Many may be desperately trying to feel the connection and do not seem to have any connection at all.

Sometimes cameras can capture orbs or light images that are not visible to us. There are definite symbols here as little reminders for people who want to know their loved one is around.

I have heard countless stories from people who have a particular animal that will appear and have an unusual interest in them where this has not occurred before the death of a loved one. These animals include cardinals, eagles, hummingbirds, dragonflies, and butterflies just to name a few. The person may feel the vibrational frequencies of the loved one, and the loved one's light or energy can maneuver the small animals in their direction through quantum entanglement. Small children may be able to identify the spirit energy that is there directing the animal to get your attention. Remember how quantum entanglement works? It allows us to better understand how the spiritual energy is giving us a sign of peace of the soul's transformation.

Pennies from Heaven

An anonymous quote read, "When an angel misses you, they toss a penny down . . . sometimes to cheer you up, to make a smile out of your frown. So, don't pass by that penny when you are feeling blue; it may be a penny from heaven that an angel tossed down to you."

Feathers

Feathers represent a connection to the spiritual realms and divinity. The powerful meaning behind the feather is the connection between God the creator and the bird from which it comes from. It represents trust, honor, strength, wisdom, power, and freedom. Feathers have been a symbol across many cultures. In the Native American culture, the feather is a symbol of high honor.

The white owl symbolizes change, transformation, and inner wisdom. The transformation includes the cycle from birth to death, leading to spiritual evolution. Prayer owls are created as the guardian of our written prayers to God. A feather can be a subtle way for a guardian angel to let you know they are nearby as their wings are also feather-like.

Children

Children often have a gift for seeing what adults can't. Listen to what children are saying. Do not be afraid. You can use this opportunity to tell your loved ones you love them or even ask questions. They may or may not respond but at least you will know they are close. Try taking a picture in the spot a child says your loved one is. You just might be lucky and get a glimpse for yourself.

CHAPTER 15

Angels and Spirits at the Time of Death

In 2003, I offered my nursing experience to my husband's family to help keep the out-of-pocket medical cost down from hospice. I am incredibly blessed to have had so many health care professionals in my immediate family. It is sometimes terrifying and sad to think about what others may go through without an advocate guiding them. I had the feeling that angels were coming for my father-in-law that night and stayed up, sitting in the rocking chair next to him until he took his last breath. He died on December 11, 2003. I went to wake up his wife, my husband, and the rest of his family, sharing that he had passed. In the back bedroom hung an antique wooden clock, that hadn't worked for a long time. On the night of his death, the antique clock started working! The clock ran for seven days until it stopped again. It made me wonder about the energy transfer that occurred at the time of my father-in-law's death. What energy is significant enough to start a clock three rooms away from the living room, and run for seven days?

Coincidently, a lifelong friend of mine was going through the death of her father-in-law as well. I shared the details about the clock, and she told me about a similar experience her family had. At the time of his death, their refrigerator quit working, and they had to buy a new refrigerator. The two events happening close together made me wonder more about the powerful energy surge at the time someone dies. It wasn't long before similar types of stories began to present themselves to me.

Hallelujah

The best gift my mother-in-law ever gave her son and grandson was a glimpse of the transition of light. The night of her death was different than my fathers-in-law's. Physically, she did not have much longer to live. She had been unconscious most of the day, and her extremities began to cool. The hour was getting late in the evening so I thought she would pass this night. This time, everyone stayed awake and witnessed a beautiful gift. On the radio, the song "Hallelujah" began to play. Her breathing began to change into an agonal rhythm and her head turned slightly to the right. My husband and son were standing by her right side while I was at the foot of the bed. She suddenly opened her eyes as if someone had just tapped her shoulder. My husband said it was like she was looking at something behind him, and then she was gone. She went to heaven on December 3, 2017.

CHAPTER 16

Tim's Story

The stories of people sharing their perspective of when the soul crosses over are numerous. Tim's experience was one of the first stories I heard about where people see both sides. I've known Tim for over thirty years; he was a year ahead of me in Mortuary Science and went on to become a successful funeral home owner, providing service to many cities across Minnesota. In my years of doing forensic death investigation and working part-time as a deputy coroner in Anoka County, I kept in close contact with Tim since he provided the livery service for Anoka County's Medical Examiner's office. It had been many years since we had seen each other. Tim had moved, and I had switched careers. A mutual friend's funeral brought us back together. As we reminisced, he shared one of the most incredible stories I have ever heard.

On October 3, 2011, Tim was on his way to set up for a funeral he had later in the day. He was in the lead car on his way to Bethel Lutheran Church in Crow Wing County. His wife Cassie was in the second car, and the third car was an employee, Roxanne S. It was near dawn as they traveled down the dusty gravel road southbound on Five-Mile Road. Tim and Cassie arrived at the church when they heard a loud crash. Tim and Cassie jumped into Tim's car, to see if they could help at the scene. On arrival, they saw Roxanne's white van in a steep ditch full of cattails. The other young driver was scream-ing, "I didn't see her." The driver hit Roxanne's van in the driver's door. Tim ran down to the van as he told Cassie to press the OnStar button for help. The driver's door was locked, but they were able to open the passenger slider door. Roxanne had an abnormal labored breathing pattern called agonal breathing and no pulse. Tim was attempting to hold her head but could also smell the gas and knew he needed to shut off the vehicle. Tim said that while trying to get the van shut off, an elderly gray-haired lady with big glasses started to yell at him over and over to cut her seat belt. He recalled feeling irritated with the older lady yelling back at her to "Shut the fuck up!" He was still in the process of trying to get the vehicle shut off before it caught on fire. He shut the van off and worked on getting the seat belt to finally release when first responders arrived on the accident scene to help. Roxanne died immediately after the seatbelt was released. It was not until Roxanne's visitation when Tim explained what had happened during the accident that one of the family members asked Tim for more details about what the older lady looked like at the accident scene. He said she had gray curly hair with thick glasses. The woman wanted to show him a picture. They brought Tim over to a tribute photo and showed Tim a picture of Roxanne's grandma, who had died many years ago. Since I've known Tim, he has always been stoic, but he became visibly emotional while recalling the moment he realized who the lady was. The lady yelling at him to release the seatbelt was Roxanne's deceased grandma waiting to take her home.

Following Roxanne's funeral, a witness to the accident asked Tim how the other lady in the accident was doing. Tim said that his wife was in a different car and not injured. The witness said, "No, I mean the older lady riding in the passenger seat in the white van before the accident." Roxanne was remarkably close with her grandmother, and it was not surprising that she was right there with her the whole time, ready to take her home. Her grandma knew it was the seatbelt that was keeping her alive. When it was released, it allowed the grandmother to take her granddaughter home to heaven.

CHAPTER 17

A Gift Given

Finding out who The Mother of the Angels is began when my mother became terminally ill. Unfortunately, this happened shortly after caring for my father-in-law. During the fourteen months she lived with her terminal illness, her daughters divided their time in shifts to grant my mother's wish to die at home. It was a three-and-a-half-hour trip for my family to visit, but worth every second as you never get that time back in the future.

I had recently applied to anesthesia school when I found out my mother was terminally ill. It was a once-in-a-lifetime shot. I would have had to drop out of the program to care for my mom. When I called the director, she said to look at a grade in my first year of college. I had switched majors the first year. My last semester of biology that I thought I had officially dropped was not dropped formally! Ouch, I never even realized it since my GPA had started over when I transferred to another college. After six years of college, it took a little work to move a GPA, but another year of straight A work erased that costly experience. It was a hidden blessing when I didn't get into school at the time.

During this time, I also took in some leisure reading. I read Dan Brown's *The Davinci Code*. It was terrific finally reading some history that didn't make me fall asleep. In high school, one of my history teachers once sent home a note to my mom. "Bonnie would do a lot better if she stayed awake." Every day in his fourth-hour history class, he turned off the lights and put on a slide show.

It was lights out for me! The lights stayed on when I read *The Davinci Code*. It is about a wonderfully woven fictional character named Robert Langdon intertwined with art, architecture, secret rituals, and the Gnostic Gospels, all of which are true. *The Davinci Code* refers to them as scrolls. The book gave me an insight into the life of Mary Magdalene and the Holy Grail. The Holy Grail is not a physical object, but a symbol of the bloodline of Jesus. The blood connection is based on the etymology reading "Sangraal," meaning Holy Grail and "Sangreal" meaning Holy Blood, Royal Blood or Christ's Blood. It was fascinating to think about the difference between fact and fiction. The book is said to be 99 percent true and one percent fiction. Thank you, Dan Brown, for the fantastic book.

Spiritual Experiences

My husband was much like my mom; they had not had any experiences with the spiritual world, although both have deep spiritual beliefs. At that point in my life, I only had occasional brief moments of spiritual activity. It was all about to change as the spiritual world became highly active for me. My mom was by far showing everyone in our family that the angels from God were close.

We knew my mom's death was approaching because of the angels that appeared to come for my mother. My mom asked my sister, "Do you see the angel there by the head of my bed? Do you see how beautiful she is?" My mom was at peace as she watched and could still communicate with us about all the visitors showing up to get her. There was so much angel activity going on; it was unquestionable the angels were mingling about, ready to take my mom when she was ready, but she was stubborn! I'm sure my mom wanted to give each loved one enough time to have an experience. Even her sons-in-law, daughters-in-law, and grandchildren all had an opportunity to experience this incredible gift of eternal life shared through my mom.

It was as if the veil between our earthly world and heaven was so thin that the angels were transparent. It could also have been my mom's strong faith that kept a portal open much longer than I have ever experienced in my life. Several family members say they saw orbs, and one of my nephews even recalls seeing the face of an angel. Orbs are transparent spheres, sometimes called globes of light, and their energy is connected to the spirits. Orbs are commonly found in photos but can be seen with the naked eye, especially around people or highly energetic areas.

Mysterious Gift Given

While caring for my mom, she asked each of her children to pick a few items that held sentimental value so that we would all receive a meaningful item from her after she passed on. I asked her for the Christmas dove music box that played on the third anniversary of my father's death. It was here my mother finally revealed to me the gift my paternal grandmother had—a gift of being able to tell when spirits were around. My mom said she never had any of those gifts or experiences and thought all the things that happened to her kids was peculiar. We both laughed, and now understood the mysterious gift we had been given.

It was nice to finally have more understanding. I believe everyone has abilities, it just depends on how receptive and open you are to what is beyond your visual sight. Just like the wind and viruses that cannot be visualized, the spiritual world is present even though most cannot see it.

My mom had been unconscious for some time, and we all took shifts to be with her while others slept. My sisters and my brother had been up with her all night. My sister, Barb, recalls the most beautiful soft white light that entered the bedroom from the hallway the evening before, making a quick sweep around the room before quickly leaving the same way. This same beautiful, soft white light came at the time of her death. My brother, Al, and sisters, Helen, and Barb, stated Mom suddenly lifted her arms as if reaching up to someone as her inner soul angel left her worn-out body behind. Like my father knew he would not live to see 1982, my mother said she did not want to die on my sister's birthday, instead, passing the day before. At 6:04 a.m. on January 5, 2007, the angels brought her home to heaven.

CHAPTER 18

Children's Gift

The morning of my mother's death, I called my husband to tell him that my mom had gone with the angels. My husband told me that last night when he was putting our son to sleep, our son asked him who the men were walking by in the hallway and heading downstairs. Our five-year-old son did not seem frightened, even though my husband could not see anyone. I immediately knew it was my dad, Paul, showing off his grandson to our relatives—our son named after his grandfather. The angels checked to see if my mom was ready the night before, but when she wasn't ready to leave, they continued to make their rounds here on earth.

I knew my son's full name from a dream years before I was ever pregnant. My son would say things when he was young that indicated to me the angels were also around him. I simply told him that if anything is ever frightening, you can say a prayer or always come to me if something is scary. My son also had night terrors that occurred every night from the age of three until around eight. Night terrors are very vivid and can be scary dreams. Children have stronger connections and their ability to fully see is still intact. For us, knowing the spiritual world exists around us, it's essential to keep good energy around, as you have no way of knowing what spirit or energy is there, and some stuck spirits can be mischievous. I keep my guardian angels close by.

We were exhausted from the nightly interruptions from our son's night terrors. I told his pediatrician about them. He gave us the best advice. "Make sure he is safe, but do not touch him when he is in a terror as it will escalate it and you will become part of the dream. Instead, just slowly talk them out of the terror." This advice helped dramatically, and he knew he could safely come to our room if he was scared. After another three years, we picked out a rescue puppy to be in the home with him as he slept. The terrors and his strong childhood connection slowly faded.

Many authors say that children under the age of eight can connect to the spiritual world as they have recently come from it, so the connections are still strong. After the age of eight, your mind no longer allows you to see.

Studies are being done on GABA (gamma-aminobutyric acid), a neurotransmitter found in our central nervous system, that will play a pivotal role in suppressing unwanted thoughts and memories in the brain's region called the hippocampus. The hippocampus is located deep in the temporal lobe of your brain. It is a complex structure with a significant role in learning and memory. The hippocampus is right next to the amygdala and part of the limbic system. The location of these structures is in the middle of the brain, behind the eyes, and next to the brainstem.

CHAPTER 19

The Discovery of the "Mother of the Angels"

My husband and son came to pick me up at my mom's house in Fargo, ND. We stopped at my brother's old 1908 farmhouse on our way home. My brother, Gary, wanted to show us the two incredibly unique pictures he had discovered in an estate sale.

The two pictures were on live edge pieces of wood. The smaller oval picture was of an old church. The second, a larger oval, had three pictures pasted on the wood, with 3D paintings of trees to make it all flow together like a collage. The pictures had small circular holes through the wood, like tiny wormholes from long ago. In the set of three, the image on the far left was exceptionally detailed in some form of a religious setting. An elaborate canopy bed looked more like a tomb with rays of lights shining down through the top of the canopy onto a female lying on the bed. She had long, dark hair, adorned by a crown, and wore a dress with a cloaked gown. Each edge of the bed was intricately detailed with scroll work even though the picture had faded to hues of green and gray. Kneeling at the side of the bed was a man wearing a white cassock gown, a Bishop's Mitre (fish) hat. This man was holding her hand. To the right was a tiny girl playing the harp, and next to her, at the foot of the bed, was an angel floating higher than anyone else in the picture holding a scroll. She was wearing a long flowing gown with an outer cloak, and she had a decorative headband or chaplet; something like a flower girl would wear. On the left side of the kneeling bishop were two people dressed in religious attire.

One was a taller man, and the other looked like a woman with shorter hair and detailed lace midway down her gown. She had a long pole in her right hand. Behind her was a black iron gate where several people had gathered, peering into the room with many stone-type features. On the wall was a pleated panel of drapery and on the top, the pleats came together with two angel faces that appeared to make the shape of a heart.

I continued staring at the picture of the lady on the bed. It suddenly came to me, I said out loud I wonder if this is Mary Magdalene? At the exact moment in time that I spoke her name aloud, there was an abrupt power surge, and everything went black. Everyone in the room stood in complete darkness for about fifteen seconds! The room grew cold, and chills covered my body. The power returned on as mysteriously as it went off. We all stood wide-eyed. Each of our children came running over to us. Everyone said they had the chills. My brother claimed that during any loss of power at the farmhouse, lights would flicker, and he would have to change the fuse to restore the power, but this time the lights didn't flicker, and he didn't change a fuse. There was no severe weather in the area that would explain the complete blackout and the return of power.

What had just happened? It comes down to looking at the circumstances of why and when it occurred. Why, on the day of my mother's death, when looking at antique religious pictures and the explicit mention of Mary Magdalene's name, would there be a power surge enough to cause an abrupt blackout only for it to return as quickly as it left? All of us, including our small children, felt chills. For several reasons, this was a day I will never forget. All of us spent much of the next hour discussing Mary Magdalene and Dan Brown's novel *The DaVinci Code*.

Looking back at this momentous experience, I realized this was no power failure; it was a surge of energy passing through a barrier. This experience confirmed the existence of an energy source well above anything any of us could explain.

I looked at the details of the photo after learning more about the journey Mary Magdalene had taken to France. I wondered if the man next to the lady in the bed was Lazarus, her brother and the first bishop in Marseille, France.

The lady in the image looked ill, possibly close to death. The middle image was of an older man and a young girl sitting on a bench. The older man appeared to be in his sixties and bald—except for gray hair around the sides and a white beard. He was dressed in a suit, tie, and black coat. A top hat sat next to him on the bench. He was comforting the young girl who looked like she might be ten or twelve years old. She had a sad, distant look on her face. The man had one arm around the girl, and the other was holding onto her hands which were intertwined in prayer. She had long, light-colored hair with curls. She was wearing a long, full-length dress. The third picture was of a nun. She was dressed in a habit, with a small cross that seemed to drape over her clothes. Behind her, a large halo shone above her head. In her hand, she was holding a large black cross with Jesus's body on the cross and roses in her other hand. Above the cross, rays of light shone down on Jesus and the female lying on the bed. Could these pictures show us the passage or portal that appears at the time of death? Who was the young girl and the older man? Was there symbolism in the oval shape and the significance of the placement of the pictures on the plaque?

Once my family finally arrived home, I searched the internet for more information on Mary Magdalene. I knew one day that I would study more about her and why saying her name that day resulted in such an abrupt surge of energy. Some of these questions were going to have to wait years until I could revisit them again. I had put my dreams on hold for five years to care for our parents. It was a blessing to spend the time with them by helping our parents remain in their homes until they died, but it was a significant sacrifice for us. The only way to recover was to further my education by getting a degree in anesthesia. I had asked my mom to pray that I would get into the highly competitive anesthesia school. My mom would often light a vigil candle that would burn with the prayer intentions. At one time, I bought her a long lighter and said, "For all of the prayers you had to say for us kids, I really should buy you a flame thrower!" Over the next year and a half, I continued to light my vigil light candle and pray I would get into anesthesia school. I never lost the determination of my goal. My husband would tell me I reminded him of *Rudy*, as in the movie. Jack Rudy's character was persistent and never gave up on his dreams.

85

Mom's Music Box

After the daunting task of dividing up my mother's belongings, I was putting things away around my own home. One of the items I had given my mom was a music box of a little girl swinging on a wooden swing. Earlier that day, I had placed it on my office desk. I was walking by the office on my way to the kitchen when I heard the music box begin to play! I turned back to the living room and asked my husband if he could hear it. I knew immediately it was a sign from my mom that she was letting me know she had earned her angel wings and was still here for me, just in a different way now. She knew this was how my dad let me know he was still around, and she did the same within a week of her death.

I continued to correlate the common denominator around death that energy could cause a power outage or surge. I began to develop a theory of an energy barrier that must divide our world from the heavenly world. This barrier thins as a portal opens when the angels come down to take someone home to the heavenly plain or visit. As with my mom's death, the barrier was thin, and the portal was open for an extended amount of time; most of my family all had little glimpses of the spiritual light from the heavenly world. It could also be the energy or vibrations coming from the heavens crossing the barrier to wreak havoc on susceptible things. It is not strange that these things occur; it is just the coincidence of when they appear around death. This is the factor one must pay attention to. When I began to research my own experiences and compared them to the views of others, I found that many others have had similar experiences and beliefs.

Historically, ancient Celtic Christians viewed thin places as locations on earth or days of the year where the veil between the world and the spiritual realm diminished. They could encounter those who had died before them. Another Celtic says that heaven and earth are only three feet apart, but in the thin places, that distance is less.

On the other hand, A vortex is a place in the world that is alive with energy. These are locations where energy is either projecting out of the earth or entering the ground. Vortexes are found at sacred sites throughout the world. Examples are the great pyramids, Stonehenge, Machu Picchu in Peru, and Sedona in Arizona to name a few. A vortex may feel like a range of sensations, from a slight tingling on the skin to a vibration emanating out of the ground. Here is what I find so unique: it provides the same sensations, vibrations, and feelings around death or when spiritual energy is around. The portal between heaven and earth opens. The doorways open and appear anywhere in the world beyond these extraordinary places, really at anytime, anywhere—even as close as your backyard.

Why God?

Many people have asked this question. If God is an all-loving God, why would there be pain and suffering here on earth? What if the earthly plane is hell at times, and our real mission is how you survive it? When there is proper understanding, the pain here is temporary; it gives our soul a whole new perspective as God loved us so much that he sent us Jesus so we would know the spiritual part of our soul. You have a piece of the temple of the holy spirit within you! Your true destiny will be salvation and eternal rest if you follow the teachings of Jesus. There is evidence of this in the bible. Genesis 1, as well as in the Lord's Prayer sites, "On earth as it is in Heaven." Each person will have trouble in this world, but if you believe in God, you will have a distinct perspective of how you get through the problems that occur in life. When the pain of death has visited your life, remember that the deceased soul is now free of the pain here on this earthly plane.

It is up to each person to study all the information revealed. Why? What if the information you receive is not the whole story? Let the truth come to you from God. For much has been uncovered, and some of the secret wisdom is still being hidden from us.

"For those who have ears let them hear, and those have eyes let them see. Happy are the eyes that see what you see! For I tell you: Many prophets and kings have desired to see what you see and have not seen it; to hear what you hear and have not heard it." Luke 10: 23-24

God wants everyone to know the truth and to connect with God so their inner soul angel will ascend to heaven when their job here on earth has finished. For the spiritual souls who have died before us and followed God, they are not lost; you always know right where they are . . . in heaven watching over you as your guardian angel.

"There is no fear in love. Perfect love drives out fear because fear has to do with punishment. Fear involves the expectation of divine punishment, so the one who is afraid of God's judgment is not perfected in love and has not grown into a sufficient understanding of God's love." 1 John 4:18

CHAPTER 20

"The Mother of the Angels"

The Catholic education I received growing up portrayed Mary Magdalene as a prostitute and repentant sinner. Now I know this information was indeed false! Initially, I didn't understand why she was having such a noticeable impact on me until I researched her life. I quickly realized how mysterious Mary Magdalene was and the profound effect she had on history as we know it today. It was perplexing how a leading lady at the right hand of Jesus himself could be left out, or even worse, her character defamed. Once I read *The Gospel of Mary Magdalene*, and learned about her teachings from Jesus, the more interested I became. Digging into gospels was new to me, and an area I considered myself to be a novice in. It was by far the hardest thing for me to write about.

During my research into some of the lost gospels, I discovered the magnificent writing in the Gospel of Phillip, who referred to Mary Magdalene as *The Mother of the Angels.* It was now crystal clear! If Mary Magdalene is The Mother of the Angels, she has been sending me help for my entire life. Thank you, Maria H the Magdalhnh Mother of the Angels! Clearly, many realize her title too. Mary Magdalene Angels Statue Alter is pictured below. The second picture shows the incredible beauty and architecture of La Madeleine Church in Paris France. Once a temple to the glory of Napoleon's Army was first suggested but has been renamed in honor of Mary Magdalene!

Mary Magdalene Angels Statue Alter

La Magdeleine Church Paris France

I finally realized the true purpose of my book and understood the significance of the power outage. The dark ultimately brought me to the light, to understand more about God, Jesus, and the two Marys, as well as the angels sent by God to help us along our path here on earth. Little by little, more information began pouring in, and this incredible journey began to unfold.

Through the research and discoveries that have been made in the world today, we can begin to understand why the early church wanted to paint Mary Magdalene in a negative light, ruining her reputation and hiding aspects of Jesus's mission from the rest of the world. Uncovering the secret documents also explained why the world has waged wars against differing points of view. What if there is a way to understand how so many varying aspects of religions are correct. Peace on earth with an immense understanding of how we are all connected and equal can change the world!

There has been some progress in clearing Mary Magdalene's name. In 2017, Pope Francis took the most significant step forward in exonerating Mary Magdalene's image by announcing Saint Mary Magdalene as the "apostle of the apostles." Jesus chose to appear to Mary Magdalene, having her be the first messenger who announced the divine message of the Lord's resurrection to the apostles. Christianity began from her testimony! The feast of Mary Magdalene is now held on July 22. Bravo Pope Francis; excellent start! There is still a lot more to do. It begins with education. Releasing truthful knowledge to erase years of lies and eradicate the defamation printed for over centuries about who Mary Magdalene was, her relationship to Jesus, the disciples, and the rest of the world.

What happened that could have made such a prominent figure in the life of Jesus be cast aside? Mary Magdalene had an intimate understanding of Jesus's teaching while being a grand teacher herself and was a priest or priestess in France. She remained at the crucifixion while other disciples, like Peter, went into hiding. God and Jesus chose Mary Magdalene to be the first to see Jesus following the Resurrection. She was the first to preach the good news miracle that Jesus had risen! There is not much debate about these facts as it is in all versions of the bible today.

When did the defamation occur? September 21,591 CE, Pope Gregory the Great, or not-so-great, began casting Mary Magdalene's sacred image as a repentant prostitute filled with evil demons that Jesus healed. Pope Gregory, the grand storyteller, appears to have blended two images of an unidentified woman and Mary Magdalene together. The story of the anointing of Jesus at Bethany is significant to the role of who Mary Magdalene was as she was allowed by Jesus to do an anointing from her alabaster jar. According to Margaret Starbird, the anointing was a regular practice of the sacred priestess or temple "prostitute." The actual translation is "sacred women." (Starbird 1993, 29). It is not the modern definition of a prostitute in the twenty-first century, yet Pope Gregory's portrayal of Mary Magdalene as a sex worker devalues her message and the significance of who she was and her title in history. "In the Neolithic period, God was honored and adored as feminine throughout the lands known as the Middle East and Europe." (Starbird, 1993, 29) According to *The Lost Gospel*, Mary Magdalene was a priestess.

What seems significantly interesting is the piece of information that appears to be left out about Jesus from Pope Gregory in this story of Mary Magdalene. Jesus was known to have studied the philosophies of the Middle East. Events in the Bible reflect that Jesus understood and incorporated the Middle East philosophies as he treated women with respect. This may even be how Jesus initially met Mary Magdalene who was living in a tower. Respecting the significance of Mary Magdalene's role as a priestess or some may even say Goddess is shown as Jesus allows Mary Magdalene to anoint him. Many have suggested Mary was born of royal lineage and have referenced her and Jesus to the mythology of Isis and Osiris with a similar set of circumstances. Isis protected women, children and healed the sick. Jesus clearly was ok with this as he is noted to have invited people in the house of Simon at Bethany as he was anointed for burial. (Mark 14:8, Matt. 26:12)

The change begins in the writings of the Christian patriarchs, most notably in the fifth-century saints, Augustine (354-430) and Jerome (342-420), who began to view women as morally and spiritually inferior to men. The material world, flesh, the devil, and women were lumped together as a source of evil that kept men from attaining spiritual union with God. The married priests were eventually run out of the church in Rome. (Starbird 1993, 68) Celibacy was now a requirement to become a priest. We can now see where Pope Gregory's sermon defaming Mary Magdalene got its roots and so much history went awry.

The Gospels of Thomas, Phillip, and Mary favors a personal relationship with understanding Jesus and God's message to the world. The status of Mary and her connection to Jesus in many of the lost gospels gravely undermines the Roman church bureaucracy. Even with the updated information, if you research Mary Magdalene in Catholic literature, the old dogma that ruined her reputation in the first place is still prevalent! Why?

The glass ceiling of Mary Magdalene's life is now breaking across the world. March 8 is now celebrated as International Women's Day for breaking the glass ceiling of women's lives worldwide. Mary was a significant, wealthy, empowered female role model who was a teacher to the other disciples and the mouth of Jesus following the crucifixion. However, it did not fit well within the male-dominated culture built by the Roman Empire nor the Roman Catholic Church. Over time, the church began to disempower her, and women's status in general. The past is not pretty; lies have been told, and wars waged to destroy documentation.

The truth about Jesus and Mary Magdalene's connection with God is simple. Jesus encouraged the literate people to write down and share his message with others. This explains the multiple writings and gospels found through archaeological excavation, while others have shaped the variety of religions we have in the world today. The Gospel, according to Mary, was immediately considered a Gnostic teaching. Gnosis means knowledge from experience, especially spiritual experience or beyond the five senses. The work is sophisticated and deeply symbolic, and the importance can be comprehended when applied to one's own life experiences. The writer of the Gospel of Mary recognized that Mary Magdalene was an enlightened authority on Jesus's teachings. Mary could use her status to teach and explain experiences Jesus had conveyed about how to connect to God. It is here where the problem begins. Mary had mastered Jesus's teaching and became a threat to Peter and the Roman Church.

The documents are slowly being found! A Coptic manuscript with the Gospel of Mary, the Apocryphon of John, and the Sophia of Jesus Christ dating back to the second century was originally written in Greek. The Codex was likely copied and bound dating back to the fourth or fifth centuries. The Codex was unearthed in Akhmim, Egypt. It was called the Berlin Codex. In 1896, Dr. Carl Reinhardt bought the manuscript in Cairo, Egypt. The Gospel of Mary should have nineteen pages, but pages one to six and eleven to fourteen are missing entirely.

According to the Gospel of Mary, "Be in harmony . . . If you are out of balance, take inspiration from manifestations of your true nature. Those who have ears, let them hear." After saying this, the Blessed One greeted them all, saying: "Peace be with you—may my peace arise and be fulfilled within you! Be vigilant and allow no one to mislead you by saying, 'Here it is!' or, 'There it is!' For it is within you that the son of man dwells. Go to him, for those who seek him, find him. Walk forth and announce the gospel of the kingdom."

Mary tells the other disciples, "I had a vision of the Teacher, and I said to him, Lord, I see you now in this vision. And he answered, "You are blessed, for the sight of me does not disturb you. There where is the nous, lies the treasure." (In the ancient world, the nous was the finest point of the soul, common sense, and intellect of your inner soul angel is here in the spiritual realm). "Then I said to him: Lord, when someone meets you in a moment of vision, is it through the soul that they see, or is it through the Spirit?" (Pneuma is the vital spirit energy, or creative force of a person). "The teacher answered, 'it is neither through the soul nor the spirit, but the nous between the two which sees the vision, and it is this which . . ." (LeLoup 2002, 31) The following pages are ripped out!

In December of 1945, another discovery was made near Nag Hammadi, Egypt. The Gospels of Phillip and Thomas, dating back to the third century, and totaling fifty-two lost and buried Gospels were uncovered. Part of the gift of connection has been restored, while the other pages have been stolen.

"So have no fear of them; for nothing is covered up that will not be uncovered, and nothing secret that will not become known." Matthew 10:26

The Meaning of the Nous Jesus shared with Mary

The Vesica Piscis is a type of lens but means "bladder of the fish." In Latin it is mandorla, meaning "almond." The vesica piscis is considered a mathematical shape used in sacred geometry. The shape is formed by intersecting two circles so that the center of each circle lies on the perimeter of the other. The shape of overlapping circles looks like a pointed oval, eye, lens or even the body of a fish. A vertical lens symbolizes femininity, fertility, seed, the vulva, and womb, which gives the light of life and mitosis (a single egg cell divides, resulting in two identical cells.)

The Gospel of Thomas tells us about the light in the very beginning as well as addresses the end in two brief verses. "We came from the light, the place where the light generated itself and established itself and has been made manifest in their image." "We are its children." (Taussig 2013, 12) Clearly, he is talking about mitosis in this conversation and one of the shapes through the process of mitosis is the vesica piscis. His followers said to Jesus "Tell us how our end will be." Jesus said: "Have you discovered the beginning that you ask about the end? For, in the place where the beginning is, there the end will be. Blessed is the one who takes a stand in the beginning. That one will know the end and will not experience death." (Taussig 2013, 16)

Suppose we apply the vesica piscis shape about Mary's question to Jesus in the Gospel of Mary. One circle would be the spirit (pneuma), vital energy, and creative force. The second circle would be the soul (psyche). The overlapping shape or pointed oval would be the answer Jesus gave to Mary. The nous is the most delicate point of the soul's energy. The invisible animating entity occupies the physical body. It is this area that sees the vision. (LeLoup 2002, 31) Applying the vesica piscis principle to the brain, we realize that the brain has right and left hemispheres, and the center between the two hemispheres is the human body's control center, the vital energy of each person's life is housed here in the mind's eye where our inner soul angel thrives.

153

The Greeks and Pythagoras believed "numbers are the language of the universe" and referred to the vesica piscis as "the doorway of life" and "the matrix."

Gematria is an alphanumeric code assigning a numerical value to a name or phrase according to its letters. Gematria coding is done so the numbers can be interpreted precisely as they are intended in the future. Gematria was used among the Greeks when writing the New Testament. It was a way the Greeks used mathematics and deliberate spellings or misspellings to ensure the understanding of secret principles. It forms a code; the vesica piscis is one of the sacred mysteries.

In Greek gematria, Maria the "H Magdalhnh" = 153. This refers to Mary Magdalene's title as a Great Goddess of the ancient world and not related to her place of birth. In the Old Testament, ONLY ONE name adds up to precisely 153, Mary Magdalene. Biblical scholars have noted that women in the gospels are identified by their name and title of wife, mother, or sister of a man. It is ONLY Mary the H Magdalhnh who has a distinctive title. To figure this out we must dive into the dogma that just because something is repeated over time doesn't mean that it is true.

Starbird takes us back in time in *Mary Magdalene Bride in Exile.* By citing Flavius Josephus, a first-century Jewish author of *The Jewish War.* It is in this documentation the town now called Migdol (Magdala) reflects the significance of "tower" in Hebrew. The town actually was known for over 200 years as Taricheae; Roman records dating back to 43 CE as evidence. Taricheae was destroyed for worshipping idols often characterized as prostitution. In addition, there are two or three different cities related to the name Migdol. The fascinating piece is how Christians would adopt the birthplace of Mary Magdalene from a town destroyed for immortality and prostitution. Once the smoke and mirrors are removed, there is evidence to call BULLSHIT! The town currently referenced as her hometown was called Taricheae when Mary Magdalene was alive on this earth. Her name obviously did not come from this town. One can now see how calculated these changes in history were back in the fourth and fifth centuries.

'God's number is 26' G=7 O=15 D=4 (7+15+4=26) The sum of 1 through 26 is 351. The number 153 is shorthand or the reverse of 351. Using a basic system where a=1, b=2, and c=3.

The vesica piscis is associated with 153 as it is the canon of Greek Geometers. In ancient times, a common expression for pi was 22/7. The formula is Pi 22/7 times the square of the radius (7x7=49) 22/7x49 is 154. Pi is commonly viewed in the decimal version of 3.14. 3.14 x 49 =153.86. Greek Gematria of her title H Magdalhnh adds up to 153. (Starbird website Sacred Union in Christianity)

The connection to Mary Magdalene's feast day of 7/22 arose from her conversation with Jesus regarding how she saw her vision. Her title is within the vesica piscis and Mary Magdalene is one of the sacred mysteries. She performed the anointing of Jesus before and after the crucifixion. Anointment was an act of divine grace. The person performing this act became a supreme mediator between God and the creation of a king. Revealing her title and role. Now we can honor Mary Magdalene for who she really was, her title, her role, and the sacred event she performed in the anointing of Jesus at the town of Bethany. She is the Mother of the Angels.

The Vesica Piscis

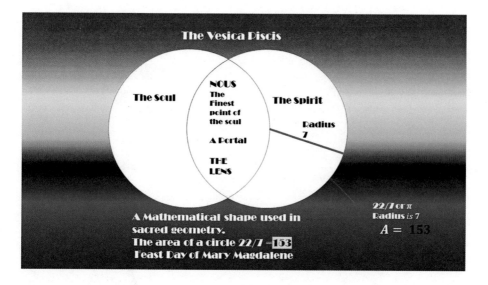

97

33

Angel number thirty-three is a sign from your guardian angel, it is a biblical number. It represents a higher degree of spiritual awareness as Jesus was thirty-three years old in 33 CE at the crucifixion. These three groups of thirty-three are vital as they represent three parts of the trinity; when it appears twice it is a master number that shows you are on the verge of a creative break-through with the help of the Holy Trinity. It is a sign that taking more risks will enable you to achieve more goals and move forward faster in your life path. Pursue your dreams, believe in yourself, and keep those who love and support you close. Thirty-three means that it is time to start sharing your talents with the rest of the world. Spiritual angel number thirty-three lets you know that the angels have heard your prayers and help is on its way! Alleluia.

CHAPTER 21

The Adventure Begins

A lot of time has transpired between 2007 to when this adventure started to take off. Asking my brother Gary and his family for the pictures he had purchased back in 2007 was the best place to start. After picking up the pictures from Jenifer, I had multiple people trying to help me locate where the church or any of the pictures were originally from. On a separate, but much smaller piece of wood was a picture of a large cathedral church. On the bottom, in tiny print, was the only clue to where these pictures originated. Lelong 82 Rue Miranmont, Amiens. Amiens is a city and commune in northern France. Amiens means "God is great." My nephew, Mike, was finally able to locate the church. It is the Basilica of Notre-Dame de Brebieres in Albert, France. Bishop Godin is in the picture as well. The pictures Mike found seemed to look newer than the one on the original wood. On the peak of the cathedral is a golden statue of the Blessed Virgin Mary holding up baby Jesus above her head. This church's amazing piece of history takes place on January 15, 1915, when a shell hit the Basilica of Notre dame in WWI.

The church's steeple had a golden blessed Virgin Mary statue holding baby Jesus out front of her. After the attack, the Virgin Mary and baby Jesus had slumped to a near-horizontal position but did not fall from the explosion. It remained this way for all the British soldiers to see who fought at the battle of Somme. Albert was three miles from the front lines. The statue remained in this position for over three years as a reminder of hope for the soldiers until

April of 1918 when further shelling destroyed the tower and steeple of the church. The 1885-95 church replica was rebuilt, including a replica of Roze's original design and a war memorial designed by Roze featuring an image of the leaning Blessed Virgin Mary.

Basilica of Notre-Dame de Brebieres in Albert, France

France

I knew France held the key as all the research indicated that Mary Magdalene, her family, and friends had come to the shores on the coast of Gaul. France was initially called Gaul by the Romans, who gave the name to the entire area where the Celtics lived. This area included France, Belgium, Germany, Switzerland, and parts of the Netherlands. The southern part of France is now called Saintes-Maries-de-la-Mer in Camargue. On May 24 they hold a festival celebrating the feast of The Two Marys and the feast of Saint Sarah, also known as Sara-la-Kali, the patron saint of the Roman people. Camargue crosses are everywhere! The Camargue cross is an emblem formed with a Latin cross. The cross at the top with the three-pronged fork stands for faith, the anchor is hope, and the heart is the love of the two Marys; a love that changes everything, a love that never fails, and a love that will replace fear. (Picture of the cross is on the red egg located on the back cover of the book.)

"Three things will last forever - faith, hope, and love, but the greatest of these is LOVE." 1 Corinthians 13:13

The Blessed Virgin Mary, Phillip, Mary Magdalene, her brother Lazarus, and other followers of Jesus traveled to Marseille, France, located on the Mediterranean Sea. Lazarus became the first bishop of Marseille, France. Mary Magdalene eventually traveled to Aix-en-Provence, twenty miles North of Marseille. Here, she was a priestess, teaching of a loving God to this region. One version of Mary's later life says she stayed in a cave in La Sainte-Baume where she spent her time in prayer while being raised by the angels each day to visit Jesus.

The Red Easter Egg

Mary Magdalene was beautiful with auburn hair and usually dressed in red. She was known to be a wealthy woman. In her journey to tell the world about the miracles and good news of Jesus, she traveled to Rome. It is here she was able to meet with Tiberius Caesar. A large audience had surrounded her before she spoke with him. On this day, it was customary to bring a gift to the emperor. Mary Magdalene held up an egg, white as snow, proclaiming, "Christ has Risen!" Tiberius Caesar mocked Mary Magdalene and said that Jesus had no more risen than the white egg in your hand is red. The egg immediately began turning into a beautiful bright red in Mary's hand. This witnessed miracle is why we have red, and other colored Easter eggs as a symbol of the new life rising from a sealed tomb even before Christianity eggs symbolized creation, spring, and rebirth. It's interesting we don't hear about Mary Magdalene's first miracle, but a lot of people celebrate the tradition of coloring Easter eggs. This is the start of Mary's testimony that Jesus has risen.

"My Church" or "Crypts"

Although I knew the pictures were from France—plus Mary lived her final days in France—it was not clear to me the exact intention of all this information, and my writing began to stall. People come in and out of our lives for a reason. And it was not long until I met a special friend, Beth, who is gifted at receiving messages from pictures through words, and my writing took a new turn. On December 2, 2020, I invited this beautiful young lady over to my home to see if any information was attached to the pictures I was looking at on the day of my mother's death. I shared no information about my experiences, or who I thought might be in the image until she had the opportunity to feel and share with me what came to her at that exact moment. A prominent angel showed up, she said the woman came from a high status, and these words became apparent: "Thank you, my church or crypts." I believe the angel's message to mean where the remaining pages of the Gospel of Mary are being stored or hidden. They are already in the world waiting for the right moment to be released by some extraordinary person. Beth shared with me her journey and some of the guidance she received. I then shared my story regarding Mary Magdalene. I asked if the email sent to the church was enough or if writing the book was my direction. The one thing she did say was that if I do decide to write a book, be aware of anyone who will want to change the book's focus. My answer was clear, write the book and see where the story leads me.

My quest to discover the mystery lady on the wooden picture was still a focus, gathering complete angel stories, and putting together the outline of events occurring. On December 14, 2020, I sent off photos of the wooden pictures to a friend, Marnie. She believed her cousin, Nancy, an art historian, might help me identify the mystery lady in the old pictures. Baffled, I sent the pictures off to her. It was fantastic! The very next day, I finally had the answer. It was not

Mary Magdalene, but St. Theresa Little Flower. Nancy sent me a color picture of the death bed St. Theresa lay on, it was identical to the bed frame. However, the one I have is much more elaborate on the wooden pictures. What was the purpose of adding to the original scene and the rays that seem to suggest a portal for Jesus and the lady in the photo? The center picture was St. Theresa at the age of thirteen with her father, and the picture to the right was her as a nun.

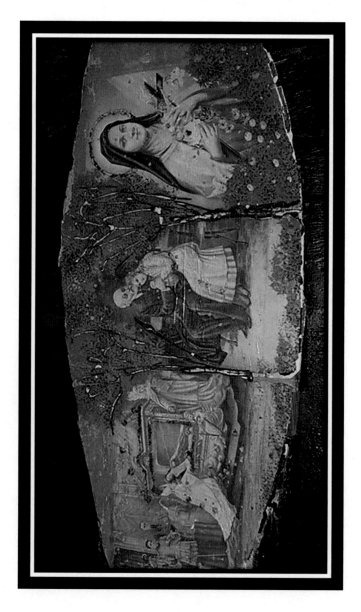

I felt perplexed as I learned that the individual's identity was St. Theresa. I wondered about the possibility of purposeful symbolism to Mary and Jesus's life, mainly as she lived in France and why was so much extra detail drawn into these pictures? I was simply unsure of the direction or end of my story or even if this was part of my book. I decided the only way to know was to continue to pray for guidance. Each night, I prayed about what this meant and my next step or conclusion in this book. After about a week, I woke up with the name Sylvia Browne.

My personal belief is to let life play out naturally, but I also questioned why I woke up with her name. I decided I needed additional help deciphering what and why the power went out when I said Mary Magdalene's name on January 5, 2007. I decided to see if she could guide me to the answers about Mary. I googled Sylvia Browne only to find out that her beautiful soul went to heaven on November 20, 2013. I remembered what a friend had said about a book of tools to help guide. I searched for books written by Sylvia Browne. As I scrolled through the many titles, there it was! Holy shit! A book written by Sylvia Browne called *The Two Mary's*! Thank you, God, for answering my prayers! I later spoke with my friend asking her who she was originally recommending regarding the book on tools? She said I recommended getting a book regarding tools by Echo Bodine. WOW, how did Sylvia Browne come to me, it is simply astonishing! We talked about coincidences, and Beth's reply was there are no coincidences.

What is the controversy that surrounded Mary Magdalene, and why would someone try to keep such a beautiful gift from God from all of us? I am asking you to keep an open mind here, as you might be as shocked as I was if you don't live in a region filled with a rich history. When saying *open mind,* I mean to view the other perspective, but not to change your belief system, instead, to understand another point of view. What if portions of all the different religious teachings are correct! When I mean all, I mean all except for the pieces changed or manipulated by man or narcissists who want you to believe that only through "them" will you reach heaven. It explains the past wars of the holy inquisition. At the time of the crucifixion of Jesus, the people's conscious mind could not understand what had occurred right in front of them. To the people who watched the Crucifixion, Jesus died that day on the cross. He was buried, and on the third day, he had risen! In the Bible, Jesus made eight appearances after the crucifixion. In numerology, the number eight means hope, new horizons, and a bright future.

The world contains many mysteries put forth by God. "Yes, I can see now that I was in error . . . Who has put wisdom in the inward parts, or given understanding to the mind?" Job 38:36

It is God, and each of us is implanted with a small fraction of his wisdom. Thus, we will never completely understand his ways, and we will never out-smart God with our wisdom!

CHAPTER 22

Signs and Heavenly Portals

The journey for the proof continued as I rented an apartment in a small town where I was doing independent practice work at the hospital. I wanted the opportunity to have more time to finish my book. There were three black and white skyline pictures as I entered the cute apartment on the wall next to the door. I zeroed in on the middle of three pictures: Marseille, France, Portugal, and Thailand. I knew immediately when I saw the sign of Marseille, France, and the coordinates of the city that I was in precisely the right place at the right time for the unfolding of my story. Marseille was where all versions of Mary Magdalene's life stories said she eventually traveled to following the Crucifixion. In Thailand, the angels had saved the animals and others from the deadly tsunami, but I didn't know if there was any significance to Portugal.

On my first day at this beautiful hospital in February 2021, I met Darcy who is an RN. She shared the story of her husband, Toby, a paramedic who had been called to the scene of a patient in full cardiac arrest shortly before midnight on the night of January 6, 2021. Toby called the patient's time of death shortly before midnight. Afterward, Toby became lightheaded and went unresponsive. The EMTs working with Toby now began working on him. He was shocked twice, waking up enough to say some words, and then became unresponsive again. The EMTs brought him to the ER, where the physician pronounced Toby's time of death at 12:19 a.m. Darcy's grief was incredibly raw; I had such empathy knowing just how painful the ache of loss is. I decided to share some of the stories and let her know I was writing a book about how close our angels are. Before this point, I kept the book and its details to immediate family and friends. In the August of 2021, Darcy asked me for some advice on receiving signs from Toby or knowing when he might be coming around. She admitted she was feeling frustrated that she had not received anything so far. I suggested she get a music box as both my parents let me know their spirit was still watching over me and discussed my theory on vibrational frequencies. I also told Darcy to take pictures in the area to capture something her eyes were not allowing her to see.

Portugal

It was not until June 2021, that I realized the significance behind the Portugal sign in the apartment until after my brother, Gary, called me, telling me to watch the story of *Fatima*. He is the same brother who bought the pictures, and it was the power that went out in his old farmhouse. He said to pay particular attention to dates and the story's ending but would not tell me why. The story of *Fatima* takes place in Fatima, Portugal, where the Lady of the Rosary appears to three children on May 13, 1917. The beautiful lady dressed in white had shining rays of clear, intense light beaming around her as she told three children she was from heaven. The lady instructs the children to pray with the rosary beads every day to bring peace to the world by ending WWI. She also instructs them to return to this very spot simultaneously for six consecutive months on the thirteenth of each month. Lucia Santos is the primary spokesperson of the children. On June 13' 1917, Lucia asked the Lady of the Rosary if she and her cousins would go to heaven when they died. She replied, "Yes, I shall take Francisco and Jacinta soon, but you will remain longer since Jesus wishes you to make me known and loved on earth."

Lucia indicated that around noon on July 13, 1917, the Lady of the Rosary entrusted them with three secrets. The date that stuck out to my brother was July 13. Ironically, this is the date of my birthday. There were three prophesies given to the children. The first prophecy was the prediction of World War II, the second was the rise and fall of the Soviet Union, and the third was a secret Lucia had turned over to the Vatican and remained a secret until 1985. In 1928 Lucia de Jesus committed to religious life as she entered the Carmel of Saint Theresa in Coimbra, Portugal. Finally, the connection to Saint Theresa, *The Two Mary's*, and all the signs!

The third secret prophecy predicted the assassination attempt on the Pope's life. On May 13, 1981, precisely sixty-four years to the day, the Lady of the Rosary appeared to the children in Fatima, and the third prophecy came true. A Turkish man fired four shots in an assassination attempt on Pope John Paul II's life. The Pope acknowledged he witnessed how the motherly hands guided the bullet's path that would spare his life from the gunshot wound. The Pope went to visit Fatima after he fully recovered in the hospital. Pope John Paul II visited the Basilica of Our Lady of the Rosary, also known as the Chapel of the Apparitions, was built to mark the exact location. The angel's motherly hands saved Pope John Paul II's life, identical to Elizabeth's story of the angel's hands who saved her life. The transcendent abilities of our angels to protect us are being shown repeatedly. Pope John Paul II is said to have gratefully given the bullet that struck him to the chapel where the Lady of the Rosary shared this prophecy to the children.

On October 13, 1917, during the sixth visit to the children, 70,000 people gathered in Fatima, amongst them was the three children. The children asked her who she is, and her reply was The Lady of the Rosary. She told them the war will be over soon and to look for a sign because she will show them that she is real. The proof she gave the crowd was an extraordinary event called The Miracle of the Sun. Seventy thousand people saw the sun spinning in the sky, changing the colors of the rainbow, and varying in size for about ten minutes. This event was witnessed by people up to twenty-five miles away. What the witnesses saw was the rainbow portal of the lady of the Rosary. The portal is how she arrived to see the children. Only the three children were able to see the lady of the Rosary and only on the last day did the lady of the Rosary display the rainbow portal for all to see. WWI ended and the story gives validation to the power of prayer! Fatima is one of the greatest and largest witnessed events of how the Spirit travels through the rainbow portal. This image was captured in black and white photos during this extraordinary event in history.

Miracle of the Sun, Fatima Portugal

In 1918, both Francisco and Jacinta died from the influenza epidemic. Lucia lived until 2005, dying at the age of ninety-seven.

Mary 153 - The Rainbow Portal Lens- Nous

On July 19, 2020, the day after my son's, graduation party, my sister Barb and I were admiring the beautiful landscape. We each took several pictures. Later that day, Barb sent me a picture she had taken. It showed a rainbow arching over the pool, but it also had a more clear-cut smaller rainbow line that angled back up into the thicker rainbow to form an eye shape. The view of the trees inside the rainbow was slightly cloudier than the outside, which were crisp and clear. We both felt like our mom and dad were there watching over us at the time. She asked if I captured the same images on my phone. My phone captured a partial section of parallel lines from the top and bottom of the rainbow in the same eye-shaped curvature; it was unquestionably there on two phones but each of us only received one photo of the unique rainbow amongst many photos taken at the same time. It was not until September 9, 2021, when I was finishing the final chapters of my book on the vesica piscis, that I finally realized the full extent of the images captured. It was the lens of the nous in the rainbow's beautiful colors, allowing the light of angels to travel—it is the portal. It was a heavenly sign of the sacred geometry of the vesica piscis. We couldn't see the rainbow image right in front of our face when we took the photos, as it was beyond our five senses, but we felt a sensation of our parents as we took them. If one turns it sideways, it is the same shape as the nous, which is the center shape in the symbol of the vesica piscis and the lens through which Jesus told Mary Magdalene how she saw the vision of him as written in the Gospel of Mary. Recalling refraction, the change in the direction of a wave is caused by the difference in the wave's speed. Examples of this are sound and light waves. Different types of mediums include air and water. Quartz glass is one of the materials also used in a camera lens. Quartz could be the plausible reason the camera lens can pick up electrical sound waves or lines of light, capturing images of the soul angel's energy in pictures. The picture is shown on the front cover as if you are within the center of the portal.

"Recognize what is right in front of your face, and what is hidden will be revealed to you. For there is nothing hidden that will not be revealed." The Gospel of Thomas (Taussig 2013,15)

Using my faith as the lens I use to see the world and my place in it. God's grace will not take me to where God's grace will not protect me.

"Now faith is the confidence in what we hope for, and assurance of things not seen." Hebrews 11:1

Muscle Cars

On Saturday, September 25th,2021, my husband and I were driving when we saw the end of a classic car show. It was another beautiful sunny day, and there sat a gorgeous wineberry-colored 1969 442 Oldsmobile. I told my husband to stop so I could look at it. I took four different pictures of the vehicle. I continued to a small group of people to see if anyone was the owner. A young man replied it was his car. I asked him if he would consider selling it. He declined as there was too much sentimental value to the vehicle. It was his dad's, and he stopped restoring it about twenty years ago when his plans changed. My husband asked him how old he was. He was twenty-two years old. We understood how a little boy could change the goals of restoring a car along with the sentimental meaning the car had to his father. On the way home, I was looking at the photos of the car when I noticed the second photo I had taken. Although it was a lot more subtle, the trend was presented as I saw two halves of the rainbow eye directly in front of the passenger's door proved a nous on the loose as his proud dad's inner soul angel was shining brightly.

Muscle Car

Toby's Gift to Darcy

Toby's Gift to Darcy

Four days later on Wednesday, September 29, 2021, I returned to work with Darcy. I had given Darcy some suggestions that might allow her to connect with Toby the month before. Darcy was ecstatic when she reported to me the music box that she purchased had chimed for her. I decided to show her the incredible picture my sister captured when sensing our parent's presence and what I thought it could mean. I also showed her the image I captured just four days ago around a car of a young man whose dad died. Darcy said I must show you my pictures I took on a tribute trip to see the trains, Toby adored. She showed me the front of the train—it was incredible. There it was, the similar shape of the rainbow eye, the nous was on the loose! What made me realize this was more than just flawed photos with glaring rays of light was Darcy's phone had video, and on two separate photos, there was movement inside the rainbow rays of light. Toby's light within the rainbow was there posing for her in front of the train! I now concur with Ancient Greeks and the Buddhists who believe the spirit can travel through rainbow portals of light. I was impressed by this incredible gift that had been shared with Darcy.

This gift showed me the pattern and trends of how our loved one's inner soul angel travels through the rainbow portal anywhere here on earth. Other people are capturing the nous in photos when they sense a lost loved one is near. The spiritual world wants us to know they are still here waiting for us until we fulfill our journey here on earth. BEE the Best we can BEE! Our time here is short!

Now that you have the knowledge and the eyes to see through photography, perhaps when you are thinking of your deceased loved one, you will get a glimpse of their visit through the lens that sees.

CHAPTER 23

Infused Knowledge

In the book *The Two Mary's* by Sylvia Browne, Browne shares that she has a lifelong spirit guide called Francine who helps guide her and has given her infused knowledge of the missing pieces to the story of Jesus and the Two Marys. I found this book incredibly fascinating as it explains why the world has so many differing views on what took place in history. In Browne's book, Mary Magdalene came from a distant royal family; her father was a silk merchant, and her mother died when she was young. Jesus's mother, the Virgin Mary, also came from royal lineage, and both families were wealthy. The two families shared a similar status; and had their children playing together. After the death of Mary Magdalene's mother, her father asked if Mary could live with them as he had to travel for work. (Browne 2007, 2-3) The two Marys grew incredibly close, especially during the period Jesus was away for his education. Being from wealthy families, they both knew how to read and write. When Jesus's brothers, James and John, returned, they began to share some of the philosophies being shared with them and Jesus as they studied abroad. The two Marys began to study the philosophies before Jesus returned so they could better comprehend what Jesus might share with them upon his return. They were both powerful women who grew in their talents through meditation. The Virgin Mary was more of an earth mother. People came to her for healing due to her strong medical knowledge, and food; she was the anchor. While Mary Magdalene became more of a humanitarian as she grew up, she was more into teaching the children, writing, and was the love and light to feed the soul. (Browne 2007, 5)

In Jesus's youth, he left home to begin his study of philosophies and teaching. There is not much information on Jesus's younger years while he traveled around the Mediterranean, India, Turkey, and far areas of the Middle East. Browne believes he may have been gone for up to 15 years for his studies. (Browne 2007, 4) Modern scholars agree that the Gospel writings appear to incorporate a variety of views from different regions. When Jesus returned home, he shared with his family how he had been infused and was enlightened with the light of the holy spirit. Jesus wanted to be baptized by John the Baptist to wipe away any past negativity to only have this one life here on earth. His Mother Mary and Mary Magdalene were also baptized with him. (Browne 2007, 10)

Rudolf Bultmann explains in *Jesus and the Word* that baptism is an eschatological sacrament used to purify for the Kingdom of God. Some of these concepts go back to Essenes and a Gnostic Mandaean sect, who were also called "Nazarenes." Christianity's preservation of the baptism from John the Baptist, might indicate that Jesus once belonged to a sect of the Baptist or developed his own off shoot from John the Baptist. (Bultmann 1934, 23-24)

Jesus began demonstrating his beautiful genius level gifts bestowed upon him from God. Abilities to heal the sick, practice hygiene, while sharing understandable stories and messages of one loving God. The news spread of an all-loving, merciful, forgiving kind of God who wanted us all to know how we are all connected. The nature of his prophecy was the rise of the soul to spirituality, and to win the battle against the wicked powers which seek to keep your soul entrapped in a world of unenlightenment against the true spiritual nature of the soul. It is by following what Jesus was communicating that will one day allow your soul to again ascend to Heaven.

Jesus traveled, studied, and obtained knowledge from diverse cultures and religions. He understood the connection between knowledge and experience beyond the five senses. Personal experience is not transferable, to understand it, one must experience it. Therefore, authentic spirituality is based on one's own effort to experience the truth. Jesus was doing this as he studied abroad during his training and was evident by his literacy when he returned, he shared his knowledge with his family, all the apostles, and the people. Scholars also note how the writing contained in the gospels came from different areas from which Jesus traveled.

Jesus was brilliant, to ensure his disciples were from every walk of life to ensure that the message would be carried to the ends of the earth. He chose people he knew, and who had enough strength and character to carry on the messages being sent forth by God. Jesus had the fantastic ability to share parables, moral and spiritual stories that people could understand from every social class. They were stories people could relate to as many people were not always well educated. Mary Magdalene was the one person Jesus didn't have to talk in parables to, she understood his teachings and was able to be a teacher herself.

Browne explains that Christianity proclaimed that Jesus's first miracle is at the Wedding at Cana. At the wedding, Jesus's mother, Mary, tells him he needs to provide the wine. Jesus then asks for water to be brought to him. Jesus performs the miracle as instructed by his mother; the water is turned into wine and provided to his guests. Why did the Blessed Virgin Mary ask Jesus to do this? In Judaic custom, the bridegroom provides the wine at his wedding for the guests. The wedding at Cana is the wedding between Jesus and Mary Magdalene. These details are edited out of the bible as they did not want the reader to think he was married, which may take away from his presence of divinity. You can read more about this in *The Two Marys: The Hidden History of the Mother and Wife of Jesus* by Sylvia Browne.

Further evidence Jesus was married is proof the disciples started calling him Rabbi after the wedding. Rabbi is the term used once a teacher is married and an unmarried man may not be a teacher, the Judaic law at the time was very specific. Bultmann confirms that if the Gospel records are credible, it is clear that "Jesus actually lived as a Jewish rabbi." (Bultmann 1934, 58)

Jesus's baptism by John the Baptist, the other major historical event in his life along with the anointing of Jesus by Mary Magdalene. In Mark 14:3-4 she opened "an alabaster jar of very expensive perfume, made of pure nard. She broke the jar and poured it on his head." Pure nard or spikenard is a rare and expensive perfume worn by wealthy women. "And it was Mary who anointed the Lord with ointment, and wiped his feet with her hair, whose brother Lazarus was sick." John 11:2. According to Mark 14;8 and Matthew, 26:12, the significance of this is the anointing before death was the unique privilege of a royal bride to the sacred king. (Starbird 1993, 30) Again, an act confirming the marriage between Jesus and Mary Magdalene. In historical pictures of Mary Magdalene, you may see Mary carrying a small jar of spikenard oil, which Mary used to anoint Jesus. John11:2

The word messiah is from the Hebrew (Mashiach) meaning one who is anointed in Judaism the expected king of the Davidic line and in Greek, the anointed one is the savior or liberator of a group of people.

A Sculpture of St. Mary at Vezelay Abbey, Vezelay, France

Many books and Gospels support the information contained in *The Two Marys*. Another fascinating read, *The Lost Gospel* by Simcha Jacobovici and Barrie Wilson, decodes an ancient text that reveals Jesus was married to Mary Magdalene. This manuscript was found collecting dust in a British library and dates back to 570 CE. Common Era (CE) is used by most biblical scholars as an alternative to AD but the numbers are the same. It is done so history does not benefit the Christian perspective or terminology, putting down other beliefs.

The *Lost Gospel* story retells the significance of how extremely dangerous the situation was as the author tells the story using surrogates. Here is the reference to Mary Magdalene who lives in a tower. The Aramaic word for Magdala is "tower." She eats honey and has a BEE following. The son of God feeds her a honeycomb with the sign of the cross on it. God chooses her to be the bride of his son, and receives the spirit of life, wisdom, and the spirit of truth. The book dives further into a murder plot to kill the holy couple and their children!

In ancient Celtic marriages, couples were joined together via vows and hand-fasting. Hand-fasting is where the couples join their two right hands together with or without a ribbon to show unity. The custom was also for the bride to wear blue. In the Kilmore Church Dervaig, on the Scottish Isle of Mull. The church is known for its pencil tower and the gorgeous stained-glass window picture of Jesus and Mary Magdalene. "Those with eyes to see will see" Mary Magdalene's gaze is leading the focus to the couple's joined right hands. Mary Magdalene is normally dressed in red but on this special occasion, she is dressed in blue. Images of the towers are also built into the framing of the couple in the stained-glass window. Below the window is a quote Jesus said during the anointing at Bethany. "Mary hath chosen that good part, which shall not be taken away from her." The artist clearly knew the significance of Mary's title and role in history. To see this beautiful piece of history online at http://www.mull-historical-society.co.uk/churches/churches-2/kilmore/

Several documents supporting the relationship between Jesus and Mary Magdalene were found in Nag Hammadi, Egypt. Here in the Acts of Philip: "Mary Magdalene his 'companion' whom he loved more than all the disciples and used to kiss her on her mouth." Through excavation, scholars can now study the unedited documents to give us a better understanding of what really happened, and the evidence suggests Jesus was married to Mary Magdalene and she played a significant role in history as Christianity and many traditions came from her testimony.

In *The Woman with the Alabaster Jar: Mary Magdalene, and the Holy Grail* by Margaret Starbird, the text theorizes the bride of Jesus was purposefully left out of the Bible for the safety of her and the unborn child she was carrying due to the turmoil in the province of Israel following the crucifixion. Historical events would be included as evidence of truth being given to the world. Other evidence is from Christian stories, such as the Church of the Holy Grail found in the New Testament, fossils, symbols, European art, and literature. This evidence was widespread in Europe during the Dark and Middle Ages. The ruthless tortures of the Holy Inquisition aimed to wipe out the bloodline heresy that the other Mary, Mary Magdalene, was the wife of Jesus and that she gave birth to the royal bloodline. If purposefully leaving the name out of the gospel writings was a prophecy, it was correct! I would also conclude that if there was also a plan to leave it out there was also a plan for saving and sharing the information. Hence the elaborate symbolism, coding, secret societies, and decoding of the day.

Holy Blood, Holy Grail by Richard Leigh, Michael Baigent, and Henry Lincoln reveal that their quest to answer a question turned into a journey that led them to a novel that woke up much of the world. The authors dive into the existence of the secret societies, claiming they have protected the Merovingian dynasty because they are the descendants of Jesus and his wife Mary Magdalene, tracing back to King David. They debate the inconsistency of the bible while working to find the truth amongst the gospels.

The Mystical Life of Jesus by Sylvia Browne, dives deeply into Jesus's life as well as the inconsistencies of the four Gospels and how they conflict with each other. There are so many other wonderful authors and sources also noted in Browne's books, including Karen L King, Elaine Pagel, and Ann Graham Brock. Thank you to all that have written in the quest for knowledge and truth of Mary Magdalene's role in history as the first Apostle of Christianity.

According to Browne, Jesus knew his prophecy was the Crucifixion. Pontius Pilate was the fifth governor in the Roman province of Judea, serving under Emperor Tiberius Caesar. Pontius Pilate interrogated Jesus to determine that he was not a threat to the Romans as he had no army. Joseph of Arimathea bribed Pontus Pilate to save the life of Jesus. Pilate's wife was infused with a dream about Jesus, and she asked her husband not to harm him because of the dream. (Browne 2007, 87) A plan was devised by Joseph of Arimathea and Pontus Pilate for how Jesus might be able to survive the crucifixion! However, if it was to work, Jesus was never to teach again publicly. Pontus Pilot, Joseph of Arimathea, and Judas were all involved in the plan. This would be one of the greatest mysteries that only God himself could have helped orchestrate if successful.

Jesus told Mary Magdalene of the plan but doubted if it would indeed work. During the last supper, Jesus tried to reassure his disciples that things will not be what they seem to be; we will all be together in the end. This being a telling statement if they are successful.

Christianity says Jesus died at the age of 33 and around April of 33 CE. The crucifixion site is outside Golgotha, Jerusalem, called Calvary. However, what was going on behind the scenes? Pontus Pilot had ordered minimal harm to come to Jesus. Jesus did suffer the flogging and torture on route to the site of the crucifixion. The soldiers were instructed to perform minimal flogging, not to puncture any arteries and not break his legs as Pontus Pilot claimed he was already dead. Death from crucifixion is the result of asphyxiation and or lack of nutrients over an extended period. The soldiers also gave Jesus a wooden foot post to push himself up to breathe and tied ropes around his upper arms to add support. The timing of the crucifixion is also incredibly significant. Per Judaic law, the crucified need to be taken down by sundown, and no one was allowed to be crucified on the sabbath. Thus, Jesus was put on the cross for only three hours. The vinegar Jesus was given on the cross was a liquid elixir that would make him lose consciousness. He was quickly removed from the cross after he lost consciousness. Joseph of Arimathea was extremely wealthy and donated the tomb as he knew Jesus would die from suffocation if he were buried, and ultimately still fulfilling Jesus's prophecy of being crucified on the cross.

Starbird points out the Gospels are written in a manner that suggests the Jewish authorities wanted Jesus crucified for blasphemy. If the charge were indeed blasphemy as proposed, the Jewish community would have stoned Jesus. However, crucifixion was a Roman execution reserved specifically for seditionists. The Gospels record that Jesus was not only a political figure, The King of the Jews, he was also a leader who challenged the religious teachings of the day. Jesus was also a charismatic healer who understood psychic phenomena. Jesus would say, "Your faith has made you whole." He was a threat to the leaders of the world in the time he was alive.

Bultmann also concluded that Jesus and John the Baptist were both considered messianic, being able to attract a significant following with their wisdom, and both were suppressed. John the Baptist was beheaded by Herod Antipas Mark 6:17-29 and Jesus was crucified by the Roman counsel, Pontius Pilate. He agreed the Christian gospels put the chief blame toward the Jewish authorities, however, this is no longer discernible. (Bultmann 1934, 24, 25)

The significance of the baptism by John the Baptist and anointing by Mary Magdalene appear to be captured in Rennes Le Chateau statues. The statue of Mary is positioned taller than the two stations of the cross next to her. Mary is holding an alabaster jar in her left hand, a wooden cross on the right, and there is a skull at her feet. Could this be reflecting the head of John, the Baptist?

Rennes-le-Chateau -Mary Magdalene with an Alabaster Jar

I believe Brown and Starbird's points are confirmed by Matthew 27:24 "Pontus Pilot publicly took water and washed his hands before the people saying, I am innocent of this man's blood, it is your responsibility."

Browne explains the Blessed Virgin Mary and Mary Magdalene were allowed to anoint Jesus's body and tend to his wounds with herbal medicine. Joseph of Arimathea hid food and drink in a linen wrapping if he woke up from the elixir. (Browne 2007, 91)

It is plausible if the timeline of events truly happened as written in *The Two Marys*. Three hours is not long enough to die from the effects of dehydration. If Jesus's legs were not broken and had a footrest, he could push himself up to breathe. Thus, he did not die from asphyxia, as he would still be able to move his diaphragm to inhale and exhale. A puncture wound to the side is survivable. Jesus was not buried, so we know he did not suffocate in a grave. I agree with the conclusion there was no fatal event or cause of death for Jesus at this time.

Contemplating this possibility, Mary Magdalene's relationship with Jesus, and the title she inherits, makes a lot more sense. Mary, his mother, and Mary, his wife, are allowed to stay with him throughout the time of the crucifixion as any family member would be allowed. It is also a sign of the family's unconditional love for each other. At the time of death, it is custom that only immediate family members would be allowed to mourn with the deceased body. It does not make sense they would have allowed both Mary, the prostitute, and his mother to be with the body at the time of death.

It is here I struggle with what my church has taught me. Jesus was crucified, died, ascended to heaven, and is seated at the right hand of our father. It also makes me think about the gospel of Mary where Jesus spoke to Mary in a vision, ultimately giving the world pieces of sacred geometry. If Jesus survived the crucifixion, this would be one of the world's greatest mysteries. This is one of those mystery questions to be answered on the other side or will the documents of proof be revealed to the world? Whatever the truth may be, the disciples did their job of spreading the news of the pathway for the inner soul angel to ascend to heaven. It could also be a hidden lesson in letting go of our version must be the correct one when ultimately the result is that many aspects of the world's different religions are true.

Browne explores the idea that the young ladies offered the soldiers guarding the tomb wine. The wine was said to be laced with opioids, and once the guards blacked out, it allowed entry into the tomb. Joseph of Arimathea and the others involved with saving Jesus's life removed the boulder. Jesus had risen from his elixir, was given a disguise, and hid nearby for days recovering until he was taken to Qumran. The Essenes lived in Qumran and referred to their lovely center as "heavenly" due to the peace and tranquility it offered to the people who visited. The very place where Jesus is said to have gone to "Heaven." It was a reference to the place he hid in disguise until arrangements for a safe passage for his escape to a new land. (Browne 2007, 107) Going back to theology class, the most significant error made in translation is not having the correct meaning for the time. Going to a heavenly place verse's ascending to Heaven could have easily been translated differently over the years.

The other significant piece for any death or homicide investigation is the requirement of a body or body part which in this case there is none.

There are many passages in the Bible where the disciples talk about seeing Jesus in disguise. Jesus is seen eight times following the crucifixion. Even Mary herself did not recognize Jesus at the tomb because of his disguise. John 20:14. He did not want her to touch him because he was so sore from the puncture wounds and the flogging he received. Jesus naturally chose Mary Magdalene to be the spokesperson for his word as she was his companion. Jesus asked Mary to notify the disciples, and she brought them to see Jesus. Thus, honoring his agreement with Pontus Pilot. Yet the Gospels referencing their companionship were not included in the Bible as we know it today.

Browne explores the idea that Joseph of Arimathea was a protector and the transporter of the Holy Grail! Mary Magdalene was pregnant with Jesus's child. Joseph of Arimathea arranged a boat to escape the region, initially stopping in Turkey. The Blessed Virgin Mary stayed, while Jesus and Mary Magdalene welcomed their first daughter Sarah. (Browne 2007, 129-130)

Starbird points out the earthen container Joseph of Arimathea transported could be Mary Magdalene's and her unborn child still in the womb as referenced by 2 Corinthians 4:7 (Starbird 1993, 26) "But we have this treasure in earthen containers so that the extraordinary greatness of the power will be of God and not from ourselves." The beautiful stained-glass picture in the Kilmore church clearly showed that Mary Magdalene is pregnant in the picture. Even the beautiful alter showing the Mother of the Angels suggests a pregnant Mary Magdalene.

Browne suggests Jesus and Mary Magdalene eventually traveled to see all of Jesus's teachers over three years. Joseph of Arimathea went ahead to Glastonbury, England, to start spreading the news in this region. The Chapel of Mary was later built in Glastonbury; the entrance to the chapel is on Magdalene Street. There is information here alluding to the sacred marriage of Jesus and Maria carved into stone in the beautiful architecture.

Many years later, Joseph of Arimathea went back for Jesus and the two Marys, bringing them to the Languedoc region of Southern France, near the small town of Rennes-le-Chateau. It is in this region they raised their four children. Two girls and two boys. Browne states that "Jesus took the name of David Albengentun" (Browne 2007, 134) as he hid his identity in France. Mary began teaching the women in the area while Jesus taught the children where he could securely instill his knowledge, as one day they would have to carry on the message. Eventually, the community's people realized who they were and became the Guardians or Guardian Angels of the Holy Grail!

What I find fascinating is the mystery involving Rennes-le-Chateau, where a poor Catholic priest, Berenger Sauniere, took over a poverty-ridden parish at the age of thirty-three near the nineteenth century. The story indicates he found documents in a hollow pillar underneath the alter when the stone was removed during restoration. The sealed parchments are said to contain genealogies. After notifying the bishop, he was flown to Paris, after turning the documents over, he had a sudden newly found wealth. This is a highly debated topic. I find it highly coincidental is when he decided to ultimately build a new church that honors Mary Magdalene with the church's new image is built like a tower! This would indicate that he had newfound knowledge that went along with his newly acquired wealth.

The other interesting thing about priest Berenger Sauniere is that he is often discovered digging in the cemetery on the grounds and venturing off to nearby neighborhoods around the area. One would have to wonder just what he was looking for, as many have speculated it was the body of Mary Magdalene. If Sylvia Browne's story is true, my theory would be that Berenger Sauniere was not only looking for the remains of Mary Magdalene, but he was also looking for the grave of David Albengentun, the alias name Jesus assumed. I would also suspect priest Berenger Sauniere was late to the search party. However, this theory could help explain some of his wealth if he was being paid to search for their graves.

Rennes-le-Chateau and its Tower a Tribute to Mary

As alarming as all of this may be, knowledge can also bring an understanding of differing opinions to the world. When we understand Jesus's message of one God is in fact the powerful piece—not getting lost in humankind's division of whose version is correct—we can finally move forward to forgiveness of past wars.

CHAPTER 24

Peter

In the Bible, it says Peter rejects even knowing Jesus three times. He runs and hides at the time of the crucifixion of Jesus. Yet, Peter goes to spread the word of Jesus and becomes the first pope of the Roman Catholic Church. He was eventually persecuted under Emperor Nero. He was crucified upside down at his request since he did not feel worthy of being crucified in the same manner as Jesus.

In the Gospel of Mary, Peter says, "Did he really choose her, and prefer her to us? Mary wept and answered him, "My brother Peter, what can you be thinking? Do you believe that this is my imagination, that I invented this vision? Or do you believe that I would lie about our teacher?" Levi spoke up, "Peter, you have always been hot-tempered, and now we see you repudiating a woman, just like our adversaries do. Yet if the Teacher held her worthy, who are you to reject her? Surely the Teacher knew her very well, for he loved her more than us. Therefore, let us atone, and become fully human, so that the Teacher can take root in us, and walk forth to spread the gospel, without trying to lay down any rules and laws other than those witnessed."

In Qumran, fifty-two ancient manuscripts called the Dead Sea Scrolls were discovered between 1947 and 1956 in eleven caves near Khirbet, Qumran on the northwest shores of the Dead Sea. The area is known for Essenes assembly. The scrolls range in size from small fragments to a complete scroll of the prophet Isaiah, and every book of the Hebrew Bible except Esther and Nehemiah. The oldest Bible is from an early fourth century parchment book.

It is preserved in the Vatican Library and is known as the Codex Vaticanus. A complete Gospel of Thomas, which scholars have indicated predates the Gospel of Luke, could have been written anywhere from 60 CE to 140 CE. According to the *New New Testament*, the *New Testament* was established three hundred years after Jesus's birth. Christian churches likely had complex negotiations over what early books would be included. What is interesting is how quickly the documents are labeled as gnostic gospels. The term Gnosticism was invented in the mid 1600's to label heretical items as unhealthy. The word came more prevalent in the late 1800's. (Taussig 2013, xxiv, 530)

I cannot even imagine all the prayers God must have been receiving over the years. The Essenes and others worked feverishly to preserve history, which was being succumbed to "Radix Malorum est cupiditas," a biblical quotation in Latin that means "greed is the root of evil." Most of the ancient writings were being destroyed. The smart ones knew they would have to hide or code their writings to preserve the knowledge in which Jesus asked people to write and share his stories. Around the world, these documents are slowly being found. They can assist us in furthering our knowledge of the gifts given to us here on earth.

There are two forces continually at work on our souls as we live here on earth. It is good and evil. Temptation comes and works on every soul. God gives you free will to choose to take it or turn away. Remember, we never know what temptation will look like in our lives or the people already under temptation's power. Do everything in your power to break free and ask God to help you do it.

Peter said in the Gospel of Mary, "Since you have become the interpreter of the elements and the events of the world, tell us: What is the sin of the world? There is no sin. It is you who makes sin exist when you act according to the habits of your corrupted nature; this is where sin lies. This is why the good has come into your midst." (Leloup 2002, 25)

The world has many empty souls who do not care about others as they have lost their spiritual connection to God. Sinful people murder, steal from individuals or their partners, commit adultery, or participate in sex trafficking. They work to divide the world based on color, gender, political parties, size, sexual orientation, and disabilities. At the same time, others may be making unhealthy decisions to deal with stressful situations, which can become addictive, and result in cravings for smoking, sex, food, drugs, and alcohol. Additives added to any of these substances aimed to make them more desirable can also make you sick or even die.

Ultimately, no one is ever perfect, and that is why we need Jesus to show us how God has forgiveness for us. We all have problems, but with God's strength, we can overcome temptation. Knowing your inner soul angel is much stronger than any temptation, one can accomplish this by asking God for help. Remember, our timeline and God's timeline are different. Educate yourself, stay strong, and pray as help is on its way.

How does the world deal with all the lost souls? Many more godly men and women become peacemakers uniting the world as opposed to those dividing it. Allow children quiet time in schools to nondenominationally pray or meditate and follow this with time for their creativity without devices to deter their inner connection of who they are. This same rule should apply in homes. Allow children to have creative time before going to bed and in the mornings. No electronic devices should be allowed in a bedroom at night to pull them away from their inner wisdom. Even Steve Jobs CEO of Apple wouldn't let his own children use the iPad because he was aware of the side effects to their creativity and inner connection.

"Blessed are the peacemakers, for they shall be called the children of God." Matthew 5:9

It is time to address the toll placed on the Peacekeepers of the world. Peacekeepers deal with society's ills on a daily basis. Repeated exposure to toxic events and situations can take a toll on a person. Just like receiving the news with only partial facts can take a toll on readers and society to fuel hatred. Change needs to come to the peacekeeper's process and the process of arbitration reform. The process is broken as it can result in a hurt peacekeeper returning to a job when they can no longer do it safely. Removing or defunding peacekeepers allows atrocity to move in, as we have witnessed in Minneapolis, MN. People are suffering, scared, and losing their children to murder! No one is safe because lawlessness and empty souls have moved in. According to the Seventh Beatitude, "Blessed are the peacemakers, for they shall be called the children of God."

CHAPTER 25

Apology, Forgiveness, and Understanding

In 2000, Pope John Paul II marked this year a Holy Year. The Roman Catholic Church apologized for past errors and excesses, from the inquisition to the persecution of Jews, Muslims, nonbelievers, and the indigenous people of colonized lands.

Through the forgiveness of past sins, one can move forward to build a healthy relationship with Jesus and Mary, and a promise of God's kingdom for those who follow the guidance.

I want to take a closer look at what the apology was all about. The Holy Inquisition started during the twelfth century in France with the intention to combat religious deviation. The Roman Catholic Church fought the "bloodline heresy," particularly among the Cathars, and Waldensians. What I find incredibly important is Pope Innocent III ordered the first seize on July 22, 1209, a day recognized as St. Mary Magdalene's feast day. The tragic irony is if Sylvia Browne's version of history is correct, and Jesus survived and lived under an alias in France. The name Albigensian crusade is eerily like the last name Browne indicated Jesus took of Albengentun and settled in the Languedoc region of France where priests and many other people lived. When Pope Innocent III was asked how to tell the difference in who the people were, his reply was simply to "Kill them all, let God sort them out." The people refused to leave this area of France as they knew the Cathars were good humanitarians even though some of their beliefs on celibacy may have been extreme. The top officials of the Cathars were aware of the relationship between Jesus and Mary Magdalene. The Languedoc region is where Mary Magdalene preached and lived with her daughter Sarah. The crusade was an attempt to destroy the bloodline in the Albigensian campaign, where whole towns went up in flames and killed all the citizens.

Fifteen thousand Knights Templar were tortured and executed, but many fled to Scotland and Portugal. The Knights Templar treasured Mary Magdalene for she represented the female side of God or Sophia. The word Sophia means "wisdom," and many believe that Sophia's "wisdom" came to earth in the body of Mary Magdalene herself! Mary Magdalene was held in exceedingly high honor, calling her the feminine aspect of the divine. The Order of the Knights Templar had access to esoteric wisdom and protected the Holy Grail the royal bloodline. The Knights Templar's knowledge of sacred geometry, mathematics, and engineering led to building cathedrals in France. On the top of a Knights Templar house, it often contained a watchtower with fire briars; with kindling ready to set on fire. The purpose of this tower was to notify other Knights Templars of a home invasion by setting the kindling on fire to send the other Knights a smoke signal. The Knights Templar went into hiding, but continued their work in secret and symbolism, only to reemerge in 1700 as the modern Freemasons.

Joan of Arc is the most famous victim of this area of the inquisition. Joan of Arc, who carried a banner during a crusade with Jesus and Maria, referring to the sacred bloodline. Joan was burned at stake in 1431 for witchcraft and heresy. Her last words were "Jesus, Jesus, Jesus!" Joan of Arc's trial was later nullified.

It has been estimated that more than fifty million people have been slaughtered for the crime of bloodline heresy and heresy by Roman persecutors with the last deaths being noted in the 19th century.

CHAPTER 26

Gods Favorite Number Seven

The number 7 is the seeker, the thinker, and the searcher of truth. The seven is aware that nothing is precisely as it seems, and reality is often hidden behind illusions. The number seven is significant as it is both God and Jesus's favorite number. The proof is written throughout the Holy Bible. The number seven is mentioned more than seven hundred times. There are seven seas, seven continents, and the seventh day was a day of rest. All civilizations adopted seven days of the week. Seven is a number known for completeness and perfection, both spiritually and physically. The rainbow has seven colors, and the colors appear in the same order in a spectrum.

Seven is a symbol of esoteric knowledge, secretiveness, mysticism, and contemplation. The triple, 777 represents the perfection of the Trinity. The Piscis Eye Trinity is a powerful, ancient symbol that depicts the sacred trinity and the all-seeing eye.

Angel number 7 is a spiritual prime, it acts as an "insulator" because it cannot be divided with or by, negative influences. For this reason, the power of this number can be used to build a strong, positive, spiritual direction in your life.

The spiritual meaning of seven is a heptad (a group or set of seven). The heptad repeat is a structural repeating pattern of seven amino acids. The most widely talked about heptad repeat in the news today is coronavirus and influenza virus. Can you guess what happens when you put two sevens together?

A helical wheel diagram. Now draw the underlining shape, by connecting the outer points of J and M. What form do you have? The piscis eye trinity or nous! The nous is on the loose! (see diagram below) In the human body, the leucine heptad repeat motif affects voltage gated channels. Serine7 heptad repeats, I will leave it to the geniuses of the world to explain. However, L-Serine is an amino acid essential for synthesizing phosphatidylserine, a component of the membrane of brain cells called neurons. L-Serine is in several foods that have the same shape as the piscis eye. They include almonds, eggs, nuts, and fish.

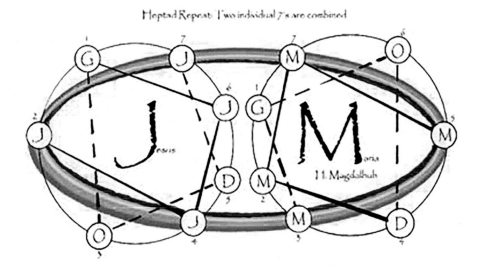

The Seven Energy Fields

Seven is also significant to Mary Magdalene as Jesus opened Mary's seven energy fields of light "chakras" so Mary could fully see. The colors of the rainbow represent the seven chakras. Chakra from Sanskrit, which trans-lates to "wheel," references the spiritual energy center within the human body. We all know a wheel is a circle and have learned the significance of 22/7 Pi as any circle that has a radius of seven has an area of each circle is 153. Recall the significance of the Feast Day of Mary Magdalene on July 22, and the sacred geometry of the Vesica piscis. The third chakra located between the eyebrows is responsible for human intuition and the inner light within us. This chakra is often referred to as the third eye chakra. In Provence, France, the historians called Mary Magdalene the light bearer!

Jesus's willingness to open Mary's energy fields may mean she could see his gifts from God! Their two souls or heptad repeats of their seven points become ONE NOUS. Half of the nous being masculine and half being feminine. Thus, we can deduct that Jesus chose Mary Magdalene to be part of the sacred trinity. Mary Magdalene is part of the all-seeing eye, making up one third of the holy trinity! We know this to be true when we switch from the Greek Gematria to Hebrew Gematria. The number 153 is the numerical total for the Hebrew phrase Ani Elohim which means "I am God." May the sacred trinity finally have divine grace.

Voltage-gated sodium channels, cancer treatment, work for the geniuses of the world

Anesthesia providers can stop pain by performing a regional block, by placing local anesthetic in specific locations. The local anesthesia works by moving inside the voltage-gated sodium channels, thus blocking the influx of sodium ions at the site of specific nerves. The regional anesthesia block prevents the nerve's electrical signals of pain from reaching the brain. In a small progressive hospital in central MN, independent CRNA's and anesthesiologists run their own cases. The group uses opioid-sparing analgesia techniques and regional anesthesia for pain management. In a workshop offered by Jonathan Kline, I was inspired by cancer prevention modalities already being offered here in the form of anesthetic choice.

Jonathan indicated cancer research appears to be leading some of the studies where the anesthesia community is not always using the most up to date recommendations for patients with cancer. Current literature supports performing a lumbar paravertebral or erector spinae block before a mastectomy followed by a propofol drip to decreased breast cancer recurrence. By blocking the voltage-gated sodium channels closed, pain, circulating catecholamines, and active cancer cells or fragments do not have the same ability to travel in the bloodstream. In colorectal cases, 50 to 60 percent of all cases will develop liver metastasis as the cancer cells can travel in the bloodstream. At times, the anesthesia provider can perform the regional anesthesia block before the surgery, thus blocking these mechanisms, and preventing the cancer cells flow in migration and metastasis.

The other interesting piece anesthesia providers will want to be aware of is the use of volatile agents and opiates as they have been shown to suppress the essential killer T cells needed to eradicate circulating cancer cells. Bravo to the anesthesia providers who are already leading the way. Thank you, Jonathan Kline, and The Twin Oaks Anesthesia team for actively sharing this knowledge.

CHAPTER 27

The Proof of Symbolism

The papal tiara was an elaborate hat worn by popes of the Catholic Church from the eighth century to the mid twentieth century. The papal tiara is now estimated to be worth 35 million dollars. In the eleventh century, the "Mitre" hat began being worn by Christian leaders. It was also referenced as the "fish hat" when placed on a pope's head. Guess what shape the papal tiara or the mitre hat will be from the top of the head to the bottom of the chin? Yes, the vertical body of the nous gives them wisdom. The wisdom that Mary Magdalene shared with the disciples and was given to her by Jesus! The information contained in the Gospel of Mary is a prominent sign used by the Roman Catholic Church and indicates they use the wisdom from the sacred geometry explained in the lost Gospel of Mary.

The Ichthus Vs the Vesica Piscis

The first use of the ichthys symbol, which appears circular, was created by combining the Greek letters that mean fish. The ichthys symbol used by early Christians dates back from the end of the first century CE. The early Christians widely adopted the symbol as a secret symbol. The ichthys or ichthus began to change from the original circle into more of an oval shape. It resembled the pointed oval or the profile of a fish with two intersecting arcs on the right side extending beyond the meeting point to create the image of the tail of the fish. Can you now see why this would be a secret symbol? Complete the arcs of the fish tail. What shape does this give you? The nous in the horizontal position, the vesica piscis = Mary Magdalene = 153. Since ancient times, the symbolism of the fish is known to be strongly connected to the sacred feminine waves of water. Water brings life; fish living beneath its surface symbolize fertility, birth, and rebirth. In current times, the ichthys symbol now carries the name of Jesus inside them. Coincidently, the age of Pisces—the fish star sign—is ending.

In John 21, Jesus and the Miraculous catch of fish. Jesus and his disciples appear on the Sea of Galilee. He called out to them, "Friends, haven't you any fish?" "No," they answered. He said, "Throw your net on the right side of the boat, and you will find some." The net was full of 153 large fish! Mary 153.

The Waves an "Air Sign"

The astrological "age" shifts approximately every 2,150 years when the Earth's rotation moves into a new zodiac sign. We are leaving the age of Pisces and beginning the Age of Aquarius. 2020 to 2022 could very well be the primary catalyst of the change with the prominent Coronavirus being a repeating heptad that is causing massive deaths around the world. A calling of so many inner soul angels does make one wonder about the significance of this phase.

According to Starbird's, *The Woman with the Alabaster Jar*, the constellation Aquarius, the water carrier, does not represent water. The sign of Aquarius is two parallel lines of waves since Aquarius is an air sign. The meaning of the sign is "dissolution of forms." The waves will be dissolving the untruths by the symbolic waters of the Holy Spirit, the Spirit of Truth. (Starbird 1993, 63) It is considerably ironic that with the arrival of the age of Aquarius, the Roman numerals for the year since 2000 and beyond, now begin with MM, the initials of Mary Magdalene. The truth is now on the airwaves, waves of mass communication, and the media. Starbird also notes the mysterious similarities of the Aquarius sign's wavy lines which parallels the ripples of hair streaming down Mary Magdalene back in historical art paintings. She notes further evidence of the correlation in the Cathedral of Chartres where the "water carriers donated the stained-glass window regarding Mary Magdalene."

Sound waves are now allowing easy education for people all over the world by listening to books. Audiobooks such as Audible are one of the fastest growing areas in publishing. In 2021 the market size, measured by revenue earned 1.3 billion dollars. The past two years audiobooks now appear to be surpassing ebooks.

Parallel Rainbow Lines in France

A colleague Jane, shared stories of her daughter Laura's, beautiful gift of having encounters with the other side. On October 29, 2021, Jane showed me pictures of Laura's travels in Chamonix-Mont-Blanc, France, posted on Mike and Laura's travel blog. In a photo captured on October 15, 2021, Laura was looking towards the mountains. I immediately noticed the image of two parallel rainbow lines. The top rainbow line was thicker and more prominent, while the second line of the eye was skinny. I asked Jane if Laura saw the image or felt anything while there. Laura told her mother she had not seen the rainbow image with her eyes, but she felt very faint and lightheaded right after the picture was taken.

Parallel Rainbow Lines in France

What seemed significant was how close the parallel rainbow lines were to Laura and yet she could not see it with her own eyes. This was identical to what happened to my sister and I. Laura and Mike's picture of a double rainbow is a rare sighting, how coincidental, but also appropriate this took place in France where Mary Magdalene, Mary 153, the Mother of the Angels, lived until the end of her human life when she was reunited with Jesus in heaven. More signs will become apparent as the Holy Spirit's desire intensifies to bring more inner soul angels home to God.

Recalling The Gospel of Thomas, his followers said to Jesus, "Tell us how our end will be." Jesus replied, "Have you discovered the beginning that you ask about the end? For, in the place where the beginning is, there the end will be. Blessed is the one who takes a stand in the beginning. That one will know the end and will not experience death." (Taussig 2013, 16)

In the book Holy Blood Holy Grail, the authors explore a letter written by Pope St. John XXIII in June of 1960. In the letter, significance is focused on the shedding of the blood by Jesus Christ. His human suffering and bloodshed should play a greater role than the resurrection and the mechanics of the crucifixion itself. Pope St. John XXIII is credited with bringing the Roman Catholic church into the twentieth century. He also revised the church's position on Freemasonry, allowing a Freemason to be Catholic.

CHAPTER 28

The Holy Grail Enlightening the World

What is the historical landmark with the symbolism of Mary Magdalene and the Holy Grail? God's favorite number seven representing divinity is prominent and reasserts itself throughout the entire structure! The seven rays of light represent the seven seas and seven continents of the world. Below the seven rays are twenty-five windows, equal to a sum of seven as 25 can be viewed as 2+5=7. The height is 151 feet, the sum is also seven 1+5+1=7. Sixteen is very prominent all over this statue. The sum of 16 is also seven 1+6=7. The torch has 16 leaves around it, and for 16 years the torch served as a lighthouse for ships at night. The torch is lit by 16 floodlights, there are four columns on each side of the pedestal base totaling 16, and the length of the hand is 16 feet, again multiple prominent displays of seven.

The divine feminine pedestal height is 47 meters or 154 feet. The calculation is from the area of a circle with a radius of seven. Recalling the formula of Pi 22/7 times the square of the radius (7x7=49) 22/7 x49 is 154. The decimal version of Pi (3.14) 3.14 x49 =153.9. The Vesica Piscis = Mary Magdalene, 7/22 her feast day. The Greek Gematria of her title is revealed by the number associated with the pedestal in which she stands. Greek Geometers knew Christianity began from Mary Magdalene's testimony and associated her as the Goddess of Love, Light, and Fertility. The "sacred partner" of the divine, Mary Magdalene. She is the Mother of the Angels!

The light bearer holds the torch, lighting the way to freedom! The meaning of Maria in Hebrew is star or light. The statue was initially copper-red, no mere coincidence as Mary Magdalene's hair was waves of auburn, and she is dressed in red. True auburn is a copper color with a slightly brown base and a hint of gold. The back of the head of the statue is covered by repetitious waves. The waves represent the seven seas and yet are high enough in the air to be seen or coordinated with airwaves, possibly the waves symbolic of Aquarius.

The torch is twenty-four karat gold, reflects the sun's rays in the daytime, and is lit by sixteen floodlights at night. Eventually, this statue turned green. We can all understand why she might want to turn green or vomit after all she has endured! In scientific language, it is a form of oxidization. You pick. Have you figured out what the statue is? The name represents her most important symbol, "Liberty Enlightening the World."

Frederic Auguste Bartholdi was a renowned artist who brought Laboulaye's ideas to life. Both members of the secretive brotherhood called the Freemasons. He unveiled the Statue of Liberty in a public ceremony on October 25, 1886. The Statue of Liberty was a gift from the French Grand Orient Temple Masons to the Masons of America. The hope was to inspire French citizens to pursue democracy. The structural framework was designed by a fellow freemason civil engineer Alexandre-Gustave Eiffel who later built the Eiffel tower, one of the seven Wonders of the World. Every seven years the Eiffel tower gets a complete repaint to protect it from oxidation.

In pictures of Mary Magdalene, the small jar she is carrying of spikenard oil, was used to anoint Jesus. The word "spikenard" in Hebrew is Nard" that translates to "light." Mary Magdalene is considered the light bearer. When a woman is pregnant, she is the bearer of the child. Although Jesus is the divine light to our passage to God, if Mary were pregnant with his child, this would make her the light bearer. The statue of liberty holds the light or torch in her right hand.

The face of the statue of liberty resembles the golden statue at the Basilica Sainte Marie-Madeleine, in Saint-Maximin-la-Sainte-Baume, France, where she is fully chained. The feature on this statue of liberty only has one foot chained while the other has broken free; it seems she is starting to break free. Mary Magdalene's freedom has been chained, hidden, burned, buried, and locked in vaults by her repressors. The knowledge she holds abolishes slavery and sexism because with the release of her secret, we now know we are all the same and have the same gift of light within each of us. This light is represented by God in the rainbow, symbolizing that everyone is equal, and free from oppression.

Inside the Statue of Liberty's pedestal is a museum. A significant piece is "Bartholdi's New Liberty." Here it is written: The face and drapery suggest a Roman Goddess. It identifies the statue as an Apostle to American freedom, law, and justice. The tablet the statue of liberty holds in her left hand is inscribed in Roman numerals July 4, 1776. The date of the Declaration of Independence. In reflection of the year 1776 if you add the 1+6=7 gives us 777! Recalling the triple, 777 represents the perfection of the Trinity. July 4, (7+4=11) 11 is also a master number, associated with spiritual awakening and independence. I will dive deeper into the significance of numbers in my next book.

Mary Magdalene was the Apostle to the Apostles and the first Apostle to Jesus! She was a Goddess and Christianity started from her testimony.

Finally, the Grail. A theory is the statue is about seven months pregnant, representing the secret bloodline of Jesus and Maria H the Magdalhnh and the secret the holy inquisition tried to destroy. The history was being preserved in symbolism, artwork, churches, and prominently here for everyone seeking freedom and enlightenment to see around the world. The statue has muscular arms, neck, and face. The garment should hang straight when representing a fit female, but her abdomen protrudes out like a lady about seven months pregnant. The gown and torch have similarities to the statue of Mary Magdalene at the Basilica of La Madeleine, Vezelay, Burgundy, France. In this statue, the light or torch is over Mary Magdalene's abdomen symbolic of the underlying meaning of growing light inside her womb.

Did Frederic Bartholdi and Alexander Gustave Eiffel reveal the Holy Grail to the world before they died? I think they did most beautifully!

Scottish Rite Northern Masonic Jurisdiction published an article The Masonic Legacy of Lady Liberty in September 2020. According to the Scottish Rite, the Statue of Liberty Cornerstone Plaque features the

Square and compass symbols of the Freemasons. Below the cornerstone is a time capsule containing the US Constitution, copies of the New York News Papers, a picture of Bartholdi, George Washington's farewell address, 20 bronze medals of presidents up through Chester A Arthur (including Washington, Monroe, Jackson, Polk Buchanan, Johnson, and Garfield, who were all Freemasons), and a list of the Grand Lodge officers. Freemasonry took great pride that their order stayed private and not shared with the outside world. However, Freemasons are now encouraged to publicly embrace their affiliations and what the Freemasons have done to build the foundation of America. (Used with permission Scottish Rite, Northern Masonic Jurisdiction)

Statue of Liberty

BEE ENLIGHTENED!!!

CHAPTER 29

Ancient Writings the Debate

There is an ongoing debate about the archaeologist's recovery of ancient writings, what they mean for our world today, and how this information should be shared and viewed in the world. Try to keep an open mind allowing knowledge to flow freely, without feeling shame or guilt by understanding an unfamiliar perspective. I chose to think about how a publishing company selects specific articles or topics that fit its main agenda. Maybe particular writers were closer to the main character or had a backstage pass to know the hidden or secret details only known by a small number. Like Phillip was to Mary Magdalene, and from this backstage pass we now know that Mary Magdalene was the Mother of the Angels. At the same time, other writers may be writing from a distant perspective or out in the stands as some scholars have viewed heavily edited biblical writings. The publishing company may select only the writings that best suit the message they want to convey. The Gospel can persuade a person's viewpoint as their knowledge remains limited to only the knowledge or perspective as given. After reading more about the Gospels of Mary, Thomas, and Phillip that did not make the cut, I began to have the same impression. They are all Gospels from the stories of when God shared a beautiful gift with the world through Jesus. Gospels were CHOSEN, and some Gospels WERE SIMPLY NOT CHOSEN. They still all contain knowledge that God and Jesus wanted us to read and try to understand. The mess begins when humans get involved; he starts editing and omitting while deciding what knowledge should be given for the world. They place fear and guilt so people think it is wrong or evil to read something different than what was chosen for them! Recall Levi's statement in the Gospel of Mary. "Walk forth to spread the Gospel without trying to lay down any rules and laws other than those witnessed."

A New New Testament edited by Hal Taussig is a Bible for the twenty-first century scholars from all over the world. They combine traditional and newly discovered texts to give a broader perspective. Hopefully one day the world will have the missing pages, and more scholars from every area of the world will put together a complete book of ancient teachings.

Now that people have become more well-read and educated, read and decide for yourself! May this book be the *sign 33* for those who hold the missing pages that it is time to release this information to the world. When 33 is turned 90 degrees counterclockwise you have two parallel wave lines or two stacked initials of m.

CHAPTER 30

Mary Magdalene Vs. Harvey Weinstein

In the United States, film producer Harvey Weinstein was planning to make a film regarding Mary Magdalene's life. However, after a series of sexual assault and harassment claims against the producer, the film fell apart. Mary Magdalene, who suffered great heartbreak and defamation and whose story has been silent for centuries, did not want her story of love and light to be produced by a person who preyed upon women. Weinstein ruined women's careers and sexually assaulted them, causing terrible pain and suffering. The strong women who came forward with these allegations spawned the global #MeToo Movement.

An NBC news reporter, Ronan Farrow, had a solid internal conviction to help these women who suffered physically and emotionally. He tells his harrowing experience against the legal system and Harvey Weinstein's pawns in the book *Catch and Kill: Lies, Spies and Conspiracy to Protect Predators.* The legal system's non-disclosure agreements have been a way to keep predators in top positions of companies. When women are not interested in their advances, they lose their positions, and not surprisingly, for some, their entire careers. Non-disclosure documents stifle a person's ability to tell the truth, while offenders continue to act atrociously. The legal system still has lengthy work to do on the use of non-disclosures that allow deceit, theft, and other ills of society to continue to prey upon unknowing victims as the truth about their sinful corruption is not revealed. It will take many devoted people to start changing these laws to save others from this type of harm in the future. Weinstein was convicted in February 2020, in New York for sexual assault and rape. He has been sentenced to twenty-three years in prison.

Strong people stand up for themselves, but the strongest stand up for others. Those who stand tall, defend, and advocate for the betterment of others can be called the true heroes in the world. Ronan Farrow is a prime example of a hero. Bravo for all the sacrifices he made in his own life to help all the women who suffered from the atrocities of Harvey Weinstein.

How do we get more people in the world to be like this? Educate yourself and teach children to know all people are unique, but everyone should treat each other with kindness and respect. Being the one who encourages other people to stand tall, having the courage to speak up and stand up to the bullies is a hard job. Do not engage in gossip and if it is happening, get off social media immediately. Having confidence and thick skin to not let lonesome losers affect your ability to shine or dim your light in this world is the key. It will not be easy, but rewarding things in life are never easy, and will build impeccable character.

Bullying is now an epidemic, just like the Coronavirus. It also spawns health issues for the people that become bullied. Signs include depression, anxiety, eating disorders, and substance abuse issues.

A bully may have underlying mental health issues, have experienced a traumatic event, or even abuse themselves. They have anger management issues, perceive themselves as being more popular or physically more robust. Understanding that bullying comes from insecure people will give strength to those who address the unacceptable hurtful behavior. Kids who bully turn into adults who bully. Adults who bully are the ones who cause inequality issues where they work. It exists for males and females of every skin color and sexual orientation. It affects everyone! It is extreme assholism, and it has no boundaries!

The National Women's Law Center are people helping remove the barriers to equality and addressing harassment, safety, and dignity in the workplace. They helped put together The BE HEARD in the workplace Act. These vital changes need to occur in the legislation system to start changing outdated laws that protect deceitful predators and the atrocities that still exist in multiple facets of the workplace today.

Women make up 51 percent of the US population but only hold 25 percent of political offices. The representation of women on corporate boards continues to increase. Globally women now hold 12 percent of corporate seats worldwide with only 4 percent chairing boards.

When we are not limited, we all thrive! Please be an encouraging force and lift people up each day.

CHAPTER 31

The Power of Prayer

The power of prayer is incredible and beyond scientific understanding. Although some prayers are not always answered promptly or beyond our comprehension of how and why, they can bring comfort to hard days, knowing one day there will be peace when we reach the other side of enlightenment. There are many prayers, many ways to pray, and all prayers with positive intentions are good.

"Do not be anxious about anything, but in every situation, by prayer and petition, with thanksgiving present your requests to God." Philippians 4:6

Most prayers consist of a petition, praise, intercession (the action of saying a prayer on behalf of another person), and supplication (a form of prayer where someone humbly asks another party to pray on their behalf or on behalf of someone else), and thanksgiving.

(1) Start with a thank you—a moment of gratitude for all the blessings you have in life.

(2) Address who you are praying to. For example, God, Jesus, Blessed Virgin Mary, Mary Magdalene, guardian angels, St. Jude, etc.

(3) Pray your petition with specific intentions. If you are not specific, you may get your prayer answered but the details might not be how you envisioned it.

(4) Confirm that the prayer is part of God's will. Make sure your prayer is of "Goodwill."

(5) Have others pray for you. This could be prayer groups or praying to a saint to pray for you. A prayer warrior is anyone who is committed to praying for others. They see themselves as engaged in spiritual warfare against evil forces.

(6) Ask for forgiveness. There is no perfect human being. To be fully human means we each have sinned. When we acknowledge our human weaknesses and ask for forgiveness when we have not made the best decisions, let GO of that sin, move forward to God's positive direction for our life. Giving back to the world can accomplish this.

(7) Thanksgiving. Acknowledge the answered prayers and say thank you for the gift given to you. Tithing or tithe in Hebrew means 10 percent Through one act of tithing, you are helping God answer other people's prayers. God promises ten blessings. In the Old Testament, Jews brought 10 percent of their harvest to a storehouse as a welfare plan for the needy or in a case of famine. The promise of a blessing is in Genesis 26:12 "Isaac planted crops in that land and the same year reaped a hundredfold because the LORD blessed him."

There is no punishment for not tithing. However, this is an area you can test God as he promises to throw open the floodgates of heaven upon you for being generous to those in need. Being generous and helping others in need is where many find the greatest satisfaction in life. Hence you are earning your own angel wings. If you don't have money to give, perform acts of kindness to others, volunteering is equally valuable to earning your wings.

CHAPTER 32

Prayers

Below are my top two ways to pray, resulting in astronomical amounts of answered prayers for me, family, friends, strangers, and colleagues.

According to the New Testament, in the Lord's Prayer, Jesus taught us to pray.

Our Father, who art in Heaven, hallowed be thy name. Thy kingdom come, thy will be done, *on earth as it is in Heaven*. Give us this day our daily bread and forgive our trespasses, as we forgive those who trespass against us. Lead us not into temptation but deliver us from evil. For thine is the kingdom, the power, and the glory, forever and ever. Amen.

St. Jude is my favorite non-denominational saint to pray to as a source of profound hope and to bring petitions to God. I was a teenager when I realized just how powerful prayer could be, and St. Jude helps in times of desperation. I prayed to St. Jude for his assistance, with most of my prayers being answered. The St. Jude Shrine websites even offer to light a votive candle to burn for a week as they pray for the person's intentions requesting the prayer. The more people you have praying for your petition, the better. A prayer written down is also a way to recall the many blessings that God has given to you, your family, and your friends over the years.

The Prayer to St. Jude

Most holy Apostle, St. Jude, faithful servant and friend of Jesus, the Church honors and invokes you universally, as the patron of difficult cases, of things, almost despaired of, pray for me, I am so helpless and alone. Intercede with God for me that he brings visible and speedy help where help is almost despaired of. Come to my assistance in this great need that you may receive the consolation and support of heaven in all my necessities, tribulations, and suffering, particularly (make your request here). And that I may praise God with you and all the saints forever. I promise, O blessed St. Jude, to be ever mindful of this great favor granted to me by God and to always honor you as my special and powerful patron and to gratefully encourage devotion to you. Amen.

As the Lady of the Rosary asked the children to pray to end WWI, please set your alarm for 7:00 p.m. each night for a minute of prayer for peace to be restored to our world. Peace and safety for the people of Ukraine. To end hunger and any other powers that work to divide the souls of our world. Finally, pray for Jesus and Mary Magdalene, that all that has been hidden is revealed to the world including the missing pages of the Gospel of Mary. In memory of her.

These things I have spoken to you, so that you may have peace in me. In the world, you will have difficulties. But have confidence: I have overcome the world. John 16:33

CHAPTER 33

Amor Fati

Amor Fati is a Latin phrase "love of fate" or "love of one's fate." It is used to describe an attitude in which one sees everything that happens in one's life, including suffering and loss, as reasonable or, at the very least, necessary. A splendid example of this is Thomas Edison. At the age of sixty-seven, he returned home from working all day in his research lab. During dinner, a man burst into his home, announcing his lab was on fire! When Thomas Edison arrived at the lab, he searched for his son in the crowd. He told his son to get his mother and all of her friends, "They'll never see a fire like this again." Edison's son was worried about all the experiments and things they could never replicate. Edison replied, "Don't worry, it's all right, we've just got rid of a lot of rubbish." Thomas Edison was not broken-hearted. He was energized! Despite Edison's devastating loss of well over a million dollars' worth of damage to his lab, he persevered to make ten million following the fire. Thomas Edison displayed the true meaning of Amor Fati.

Romans 8:28 is one of the Bible's best-known verses which reminds me of Amor Fati. "For God works all things together for good to those who love him and are called according to his purpose."

REFERENCES

Browne, Sylvia. 2004. *Book of Angels.* Carlsbach: HayHouse Inc.

Browne, Sylvia. 2007. *The Two Marys The Hidden History of the Mother and Wife of Jesus.* New York: Penguin Random House.

Bultmann, Rudolf. 1934. *Jesus and the Word.* New York: Charles Scribner's Sons.

Crossan, Edited by Hal Taussig with Foreword by John Dominic. 2013. *A New New Testament.* New York: Mariner.

LeLoup, Jean-Yves. 2002. *The Gospel of Mary Magdelane by Jean-Yves LeLoup .* Rochester: Inner Traditions International.

Starbird, Margaret 1993. *The Woman with the Alabaster Jar: Mary Magdalen and the Holy Grail.* Rochester: Bear & Company.

Wilson, Simcha Jacobovici & Barrie. 2014. *The Lost Gospel Decoding The Ancient Text That Reveals Jesus' Marriage To Mary the Magdalene.* New York City: Simon & Schuster.

Websites:

EagleBrookchurch.com

Margaret Starbird's Website Sacred Union in Christianity

Twin Oaks Anesthesia www.TwinOaksAnesthesia.com

Articles or Blogs: Scottish Rite Northern Masonic Jurisdiction: The Masonic Legacy of Lady Liberty September 2, 2020, https://scottishritenmj.org/blog/freemasonary-statue-liberty

Made in the USA
Monee, IL
25 February 2023

28656611R00102